Holy Spirit Rising
The Vital Return of Our Divine Mother
for the Healing of Our Planet

Sylvia Binsfeld

THE GREATEST IS LOVE
PRESS

GREATEST IS LOVE Press
Walnut Creek, CA 94598

Disclaimer: The author of this book does not prescribe
either directly or indirectly the use of any practice or
healing methods shared in these pages without the advice
of a professional or physician The author only means to
share general information about her insights, research,
observations, and experiences.

Published May 7th, 2024

Illustrations by Evangelia Philippidis
Cover Design and Ink Doodles by Sylvia Binsfeld
Interior Design by Val Sherer

Library of Congress #2023913391

Names: Binseld, Sylvia, author

Title: Holy Spirit Rising: The Vital Return of Our Divine
Mother for the Healing of the Planet

Subjects: Mother Holy Spirit (spirituality) Divine Feminine
(spirituality) Equality, Planetary Healing (ecology)
Hardback 978-0-9837048-2-9
Paperback 978-0-9837048-3-6
Ebook 978-0-9837048-4-3

PRINTED IN THE UNITED STATES OF AMERICA

This book is dedicated to
my children and to all of humanity.
May we find the love and the good
in each other to help heal our world.

Wisdom of Solomon 7: 7-10

Wherefore I wished, and understanding was given to me: and I called upon God, and the spirit of wisdom came upon me: And I preferred her before kingdoms and thrones, and esteemed riches nothing in comparison to her.

Contents

Contents..vii

Acknowledgments xi

Foreword
A Gift to the World xiii

Part 1: A Call for Our Mother's Return.................. 1

This Book..3

Where it All Began for Us
The Old Testament 9

The Creation of Humankind 10

God is All.. 12

Adam and Eve 14

The Meaning of Image 20

Ruah Means Feminine Spirit 21

The Fluid, Multi-Layered
Aramaic and Hebrew Languages 23

215 Manuscripts Depicting a
Female Holy Spirit..25

Names for Holy Spirit...................................... 28

The Shekinah... 30

Wisdom of Solomon 33

The Holy Spirit as Lady Wisdom 34

More Proof in Sirach 40

The New Testament... 42

The Story of Jesus's Conception..................... 46

To be a Father is Relational 52

Jesus Called the Holy Spirit Mother 54

The Holy Trinity:
Missing Our Holy Spirit Mother 57

The Lord's Prayer 60

The Holy Spirit as a Dove.......................................62

Blasphemy Against the Holy Spirit 65

Being Born Again Through the
Mother Holy Spirit 68

Mary Magdalene and Women in Leadership...........70

There Were Female Apostles...................................78

The Gospel of John..82

The Gospel of the Beloved Companion 85

The Gnostic Gospels..88

What the Inclusive Bible Reveals 95

Christian Mystics and Prophets.............................97

Part 2: The Present Day 105

Effects of Removing Our Divine Mother on
Girls and Women... 112

Effects of Removing Our Divine Mother on Men and
Boys 121

Effects of Removing Our Divine Mother on Marriage
and Relationships...132

Effects of Removing Our Divine Mother on Diversity
of All Kinds..140

The Effects of Removing Our Divine Mother on
  Nature and Climate Change 143

Effects of Removing Our Divine Mother on
  Film and Story.. 151

Effects of Removing Our Divine Mother on Politics
  and Leadership, War and Peace 161

Effects of Removing Our Divine Mother on
  Business and Economics 169

The Effects of Removing Our Divine Mother on
  Consumerism 175

Sayings According to the Times............................ 179

Taking Care of Our Planet.................................182

Taking Care of and Empowering Our Children......188

Social Media 193

The Mental Health Crisis 196

Self-Healing with the Help of Nature 299

Beauty Heals 208

Brave Young Voices Rising 212

Engaging the Wise Elders 213

Balance 215

God Energy... 216

Connecting to the Soul of the Cosmos 219

Shine Our Light.. 223

What We Do Take with Us 225

The Power of Words and Sound 227

The Power of Meditation,
  Contemplation and Prayer 231

ix

The Power of Forgiveness 238

The Power of Gratitude 241

The Greatest is Love 243

The Prophecy 247

Conclusion:
    All Together Now: Global Evolution 248

My Mystical Vision:
    We Are One with God 251

References and Resources 255

About the Author 282

About the Illustrator 283

Acknowledgments

This book would not have been possible without the remarkable investigation, research, wisdom, and dedication of the brilliant scholars listed below. Their Biblical findings paved the way for others to follow. They inspired me to question and explore more closely what I had been taught, which led to the writing of this book. With it completed, I'll go back to working in independent film. The life-long dedication of these gifted scholars, and many others, continues to raise much-needed awareness across the globe—a heartfelt thank you to all of you.

My deepest gratitude goes to Anne Baring for her wisdom and encouragement and her extraordinary writings on the Divine Feminine. They shine as a guiding light for the rest of us.

Thank you also to Ally Kateusz, Margaret Barker, Elaine Pagels, Craig Atwood, Marianne Widmalm, Karen King, Virginia Ramey Mollenkott, Arthur Everett Sekki, Neil Douglas-Klotz, Jehanne de Quillan, Ann Graham Brock, Elizabeth Schrader, Lynne Bundesen, Z'ev ben Shimon Halevi, Meggan Watterson, Cynthia Bourgeault, Andrew Harvey, Jules Cashford, James Hale, Kayleen Asbo, Deidre Havrelock, and others, for sharing your discoveries and awareness-raising works with us. They bring truth, clarity, and the kind of wisdom the world urgently needs right now.

Foreword

A Gift to the World

Sylvia has written a vitally important book, one that should have been written long ago. She points to the wound inflicted on humanity by the loss of God-the-Mother and shows how this happened and why. As she writes:

> To heal this and so much more, we need
> to go back to where it all started, the
> biggest erasure of the feminine of all time.
> Who on this planet would not be affected
> by the loss of their earthly mother? The
> removal of our Eternal Mother has left a
> gaping hole, an imbalance and a warped
> worldview of immeasurable proportions.
> Anyone identifying as a woman or girl is
> most directly harmed, but men, boys, all
> of humanity, nature, our planet, and the
> cosmos have all been deeply injured by this.
> This book is a plea for the welfare of the
> planet and all of humanity. Our quality of
> life and our hope for a future depend on her
> return.

To write a book like this, uncovering a great wrong, takes immense courage and commitment and years of meticulous research. It takes long hours of work in which the vision of what needs to be set right is never relinquished. It needs trust and perseverance, in her case, over many years.

Looking at the world today, at the tragic repetition of old patterns, the reenactment of the sacrificial rituals of war, as well as the huge challenge of climate change, it is not difficult to see that something has to change and that we have come—all of us—to a crucial time of choice. Can we learn through her discoveries where we went wrong, where we lost our relationship with Nature, what ideas have influenced us and what too-limited image of deity we have been worshipping for thousands of years?

Sylvia's book can help us to find the answers to these questions. It can help us to look around at the world and ask why people are suffering—from hunger, from war, from anxiety and depression and a sense of hopelessness. It can help us to define what is missing, what has been neglected and rejected and what needs to be restored if we are to receive the assistance we need. It can explain why we have lost touch with our soul and how urgent it is for us to get in touch with it again.

To use the metaphor of a famous and much-loved fairy-tale, we need to hack our way through the dense hedge of thorns that has come into being over centuries and millennia, to discover the Sleeping Beauty who was put into a trance so long ago and bring her back to life. This is the courageous and vital alchemical work that Sylvia has accomplished through her devotion to bringing the Holy Spirit to life again for us.

Anne Baring, author of
The Dream of the Cosmos: A Quest for the Soul

Author's Message to the Reader

Dear Reader,

If you are reading this book, it is likely that you, like me, long for a meaningful relationship with God. We choose to live deeply because we know that there is more than meets the eye to our existence. Have you, however, also felt there is something or someone missing—that something is not quite right?

It is open knowledge that the Bible was edited. My question has always been—why? How can it even have been allowed to alter the Holy Bible!? What was the intention behind making these changes?

Holy Spirit Rising is the result of years of reading and research after my awareness was sparked by a series of unexpected spiritual experiences throughout my life. This led to a bigger opening during a qigong healing event that took place in a chapel that used to be a convent. The experience and what followed changed my life forever. It also rocked the core of everything I had been told. It took me beyond my comfort zone and, over time, forced me to let go of some long-held beliefs. Most occurrences were beautiful, a few were terrifying. Though most of these experiences are private to me, there was one that I am moved to share later in the book.

I was made aware that God is both male and female. I needed to know more. I was meticulous and cautious in my research, as I wanted to be sure to get to the truth. My most perplexing question was, "Why was I never told there is a Mother God? Why was she no longer in our awareness?" Now that she was in mine, I was never letting her go.

It was humbling to read the works of great scholars on the topic of our Mother the Holy Spirit and other biblical texts. I wished I had known this information sooner but was grateful to be made aware of it then. I immersed myself in this newfound wisdom. My faith was deepened by the discoveries.

Conversely, I was overwhelmed to see the mountains and mountains of books, stating that the Holy Spirit is male. With published evidence by theologians and scholars showing that the Holy Spirit had originally been recognized to be female, why was it not accepted common knowledge?

I've tried to keep what I share here in the framework of what we have been taught and understand, because like the layers of an onion, once you peel back one layer, you discover more, and then more, and it can become overwhelming. For the sake of this book, I will peel back a couple of layers or so. It is good to allow time to reflect.

It took a few years to absorb, accept, and process what I found. I am still learning as I go, to this day. During the COVID-19 lockdowns, when my other work halted, I decided to stop reading just for my own knowledge and started to research more extensively to write this book, which took over three more years. Though I researched scholarly material, after scholarly material, along with different versions of the Bible, I am not a scholar. Therefore, this is an introductory book, sharing with you the highlights of what I have discovered within myself and the wonderful academic literature on this topic. In the back of this book, I introduce you to authors more qualified than me to take you deeper than my book, as they share their knowledge and peel back even more of those layers.

What I unearthed moved me to the core. I learned that the Holy Spirit is indeed female, and she was originally seen as such. She is our Divine Mother but through redactions in the Bible, she was made male. No wonder the world is in such trouble. What a slanted lens of perception and imbalance of energies was created, by removing our Mother God—our Father God's partner—from the world's consciousness. How has this brought us to where we are today?

Though I am not a scholar, I am a storyteller through the medium of film. After my series of spiritual experiences, I founded the Conscious Media Movement, where I encourage filmmakers of ALL genres to create films that uplift society. By using story to raise consciousness, we can contribute to the healing of our planet. I am working on getting a children's/family film off the ground, but I took time off to write this book. It feels urgent, as we need a healing shift in consciousness to save our planet.

Getting films made as a female filmmaker, has been a colossal challenge. For the last century and, until just recently, only 4% to 7% of studio-funded films would hire a woman in the position of director—and this is not for a lack of gifted female directors trying to break in. Since story is most often used to reflect life and teach us about ourselves, this omission of the female voice and the insights coming from our lens of perception, has had a profoundly negative effect on society. To heal this and so much more, we need to go back to where it all started, the biggest erasure of the feminine of all time. Who on this planet would not be affected by the loss of their earthly mother? The removal of our Eternal Mother has left a gaping hole, an imbalance, and a warped worldview of immeasurable proportions. Anyone identifying as a woman or girl is most directly harmed, but men, boys, all of humanity, our planet, and the cosmos, have all been deeply injured. This book is a plea for the welfare of the planet and all of humanity. Our quality of life and our hope for a future depend on her return.

The translators who changed our Holy Spirit to male in our Bible were male. While first making the translations to English, they appear to have been doing their best with the material they had access to at the time, so we need to keep that in mind. We want to be careful not to pass judgment on someone who lived thousands of years ago in completely different times and circumstances. We can only imagine their world. Yet, it is hard to believe that many other changes made by redactors and translators were accidental. By calling out these redactors, a male reader may feel that he, and men in general, are being blamed. Please know that is not the case or intention of this book at all. The loss of the Mother and the devaluing of the feminine short-changed both women and men. For our mental, emotional, and spiritual health, we all carry elements of masculine and feminine energies. Therefore, every one of us was harmed by the loss of our Godly Mother.

There are too many remarkable men in this world to ever make a sweeping judgment. Everyone has individual choices and individual life experiences that shape them. With God being both male and female, Father, Mother, and Child, it is clear that we are to love and honor the genders equally. We were even instructed to "Honor thy father and honor thy mother." That is the healing point I'm trying to make. The hope is that this book will benefit all and harmonize and deepen the relationship between the genders. God is all of humanity, no matter gender, race, or religion, God is All of everything there is.

In this book, we bring to light what happened so long ago to take our loving Mother away from all of us, changing our image of God, our relationship to Him/Her, and with that all of life. There will be readers who continue to believe in an exclusively male God, sincerely seeing everything in a different manner than I have shared here, and that, of course, is fine. We can honorably and respectfully disagree. Varying views are part of life, and we are each on our own journey.

This book is a summary of what I found. It is simply meant to open the door to that knowledge, presented in a bite-sized, easy-to-read style. At the back of this book, I share the titles of numerous scholarly books as references, along with an abundance of additional material and resources, to help anyone who wishes to delve more deeply and explore further than what I have shared here.

Thank you and God bless you.

Part 1:
A Call for Our Mother's Return

This is a pivotal time in history. No matter how much we would like to go on with life as we know it, our planet is calling out to us that something needs to change if we are to continue to exist here. Radical actions need to be initiated right away, on an individual and global level. But, as long as we look at our issues in the world as strictly physical, our planet will not survive, as they are also deeply rooted spiritual ones. We have lost a vital part of our connection to life and spirit. About 2,500 years ago, our wise, compassionate Divine Mother, the Holy Spirit, was taken from the world's consciousness and we are suffering the consequences of this loss.

Long ago, before any of us existed, she existed. The cosmos was birthed through her. Yet most of us don't know her for who She is, the feminine Being in the godhead—our Mother God, the Holy Spirit.

Many hands along the way made redactions to the Bible that would alter the very face of God! Mother God disappeared as if she never existed; only Father God remained.

And with that, about 50% of humanity lost their reflection in the godhead.

Women will never find true equality, so long as the female is removed from the Divine. As long as men stand beside an all-male God, women can make progress here and there, but we will never be seen as fully equal.

We also lost the deep, compassionate, loving, wisdom that comes from her, our Mother God, along with our reverence for the feminine and for nature, which was formerly always associated with her. With matricide came eco-cide. Now, she is slowly rising again. Nothing is more urgent for our survival than her complete return.

This Book

If you haven't taken a moment to read my "Author's Message to the Reader" above, please do. This book uncovers what happened in the Judeo-Christian religions which have been the religions for a great part of the population. Because of this vast reach, what happened regarding the Holy Spirit affects everyone on earth. What infiltrated those religions, also infiltrated most religions. Buddhism, for example, is historically quite male-dominated. I have not found any of its classic writings and teachings in the female voice. This book can be healing for all of us no matter our religious or spiritual beliefs because there are common threads that run through all of them.

Holy Spirit Rising is not about disrespecting the importance of the Bible. Quite the contrary, this introductory book is about honoring the importance of the Bible's initial documentation and trying to restore to it the original message and story. As a filmmaker, I understand the power of editing. You can completely alter any film's story, its meaning, and purpose in just one short edit session. The Bible was extensively edited, and this happened during a time when even a well-intentioned translator/redactor was viewing the world through an extremely patriarchal lens. This is the frame through which they made the changes. To understand the harm many of these redactions and slanted translations have caused to humanity, we need to go back in history; a history which was skewed to the detriment of women, and to the feminine, in general.

For the Bible quotes, I use the Douay-Rheims Bible (1899) version. It is a translation from Latin Vulgate (created through the works of St. Jerome), into English by members of the English College, Douai.

Later in the book, we explore how these redactions created a terribly off-kilter worldview with flawed principles. What happened those thousands of years ago and what it set in motion is largely responsible for the challenging times humanity is currently facing. Unfortunately, things may get worse before they get better. But, if we are able to open our eyes and consciousness, can we bring forth a time of mass evolution to a higher way of being, rather than mass destruction? Can we remove the illusion of separation and become unified in love the way Jesus taught?

Let's start our journey.

Proverbs 3:15-18

She is more precious than all riches: and
all the things that are desired, are not to be
compared with her. Length of days is in her
right hand, and in her left hand riches and
glory. Her ways are beautiful ways, and all
her paths are peaceable. She is a tree of life to
them that lay hold on her: and he that shall
retain her is blessed.

Where it All Began for Us

The Old Testament

When we open the Old Testament of the Bible, the first words our eyes fall upon are:

Genesis 1:1-4

> In the beginning God created heaven, and earth. And the earth was void and empty, and darkness was upon the face of the deep; and the spirit of God moved over the waters. And God said: Be light made. And light was made. And God saw the light that it was good....

And so, it began—Father God and Mother Holy **Spirit**, who are both the One God together, created the world side by side. She, the Spirit of God, the partner of God the Father was there from the beginning. She moved over the face of the waters actively participating in creation.

The Creation of Humankind

After many days of work, we now get to the part in Genesis 1 that speaks about the creation of humankind.

Note: Humankind is the word used most often in our contemporary Bibles, but in the old Douay-Rheims Bible version we will come across the word man, to mean a human being of either sex—though that is not the image we get when we hear that word. More on that later.

I often get asked the question, does gender matter and can God take on form? Here is what it says in Genesis 1:26-27.

Genesis 1:26-27

> And he said: Let **us** make man [humankind]
> to **our** image and likeness: and let him
> [them] have dominion over the fishes of the
> sea, and the fowls of the air, and the beasts,
> and the whole earth, and every creeping
> creature that moveth upon the earth. And
> God created man [humankind] to his own
> image: to the image of God he created him
> [them]: **male and female** he created **them**.

We were created in **their** image, male and female, together and at the same time, which brings a sense of equality. These words also imply that God can take on a physical presence and that the presence of God is both masculine and feminine. In the creation of both the male and female in God's image, it shows us that gender has a purpose. The genders are together in God, in companionship and partnership, as they are present in humanity.

We have also grossly misunderstood the part about our being given dominion over the earth and the creatures on it. It does not mean that we have been given carte blanche to do whatever we want. Quite the opposite. We were given a responsibility! When we are given any kind of charge, we are responsible for what we have been given charge of. We were called to be the stewards and caretakers of our precious Mother Earth and all its living beings!

God is All

The popular argument that God is a genderless, spirit being is often misused to silence women when they ask, "Why is God strictly being portrayed as a he? Where is our connection and our reflection in God which was described in Genesis 1?" The response to this question tends to be, "God is really a genderless spirit or is transcendent of gender. So, stop being petty about representation. We are not actually saying 'he' as if he is only a he—know that the female is in there *somewhere*. But, by the way, we will be calling God, 'Father,' and we will be calling him 'Son', and the Holy Spirit who was originally female we have changed to male.' But know that it doesn't matter how we label God's gender expressions."

We have been given a strictly male representation of God, not a transcendent or genderless representation. My first question is, well, if gender doesn't matter, why go through the trouble of changing the gender of the Holy Spirit from how she was acknowledged in the original language of Aramaic and Hebrew? With much of the Bible having been written allegorically, it is challenging enough to speak of God, the All, who permeates everything that is, using our worldly terminology. To then remove the feminine expressions in the original language, thus seriously limiting and fragmenting the All, cannot be a good thing, however we look at it.

It is interesting that in Genesis 1, the writers of this vitally important text used the Hebrew noun **'elohîm** for God, which is **plural**. They are not saying God, singular. They are saying **Gods, plural**. If they were using the singular noun for God, they would have written 'el or 'eloah.

They used the plural form, which gives us vital information—**they are talking about the two of them**: God our Father in whose image men were made after and God our Mother, the Holy Spirit, in whose image women were made after.

It has been contended that the plural form can at times be used as its majestic form for a singular person and that is what they chose to do in our translations. But, in context, having used the plural form in this case would have made complete sense. Even if we were to go with God in singular form here, the use of the word **us** and the words **male** and **female**, in Genesis 1:26-27 show that God is both.

Adam and Eve

Once we finish reading and absorbing this first creation story, up comes a second, whole new creation story—the story of Adam and Eve. I will only touch upon Adam and Eve briefly since the story would require another book unto itself. There is, however, a tie between what transpired with the Holy Spirit and the tale of Adam and Eve.

Additionally, I feel the need to address this story because it has done so much damage on many levels to all of humanity, including being used to prove the inferiority of women. Eve is blamed for most everything and, through her, women as a whole. That blame has been disastrous for how women are regarded and their safety and place in the world. Also, the story creates a false narrative of separation which has been devasting to how we relate to God, and how we treat each other and the planet.

The original story at the beginning of Genesis spoke beautifully of the male and female, who were birthed harmoniously together in an ensouled universe. There is an awareness of equality and partnership. There is an awareness of a dance between male and female energies. This second story is glaringly different. There are debates as to its true meaning. I am still studying and exploring the findings myself. For, I agree with what Methodist Preacher and Bible Scholar, Dr. Margaret Barker says regarding being able to figure out what transpired in the writing of the Old Testament—it happened so long ago, the best we can do here is "informed guesswork". So, let's begin.

Jungian analyst and scholar Anne Baring shares in her excellent book written with Jules Cashford, *The Myth of the Goddess*, how this new fall of man creation story is not in alignment with the first creation story at all. She explains that the Adam and Eve narrative was added later, around 621 BCE by a powerful group of priests called the Deuteronomists aka Yawists.

> Anne Baring said, "Later Christian commentators, interpreting the myth literally, generalized from the 'sin of Eve' to the character of woman, which has had serious and far-reaching consequences for related attitudes to matter, earth and nature as aspects of the rejected feminine."

Barker has written about the later addition of the Adam and Eve story as well, explaining the puzzling dilemma of having two birth of humanity stories in one Bible! She says that though the Adam and Eve story appears at the beginning of the Old Testament, it looks very much as though it was **added** as one of the last pieces, because this story isn't mentioned again anywhere else in the Old Testament! She says that this is not usual. Usually, there is a cross-referencing from book to book, story to story. In other words, we should find pieces of this story in other stories in the Bible, but we don't.

In her book, *The Great High Priest*, Barker writes: In the most ancient tradition of Israel, **Yahweh was both female and male**, and it was they who co-created the world. The feminine side of Yahweh was called Wisdom, the consort of Yahweh, the Queen of Heaven, the bright and radiant one whose teaching was like the light of the dawn."

When we look at Anne Baring's research, she has come to the same discoveries. I share all that Anne Baring sent me for this book, *Holy Spirit Rising*, with her permission. She explains here:

> "What happened was this: the Jewish people once worshipped both a Goddess and a God, a Queen and a King of Heaven, who together created the world. But in 623 BCE under a king called Josiah, a powerful group of priests called Deuteronomists took control of the First Temple in Jerusalem. They removed every trace of the Goddess Asherah, the Queen of Heaven, who was worshipped as the Holy Spirit and Divine Wisdom and also as the Tree of Life—a cosmic Tree that connected the invisible and visible worlds, and whose fruit was the gift of immortality. Her statue was removed from the temple. All images of her were destroyed and her sacred groves of trees were cut down. The ancient rituals of the High Priest which had honoured and communed with the Queen of Heaven as the Tree of Life, Divine Wisdom, and the Holy Spirit were replaced by new rituals based on obedience to Yahweh's Law."

Anne Baring continues:

> "The Deuteronomists created the Myth of the Fall (Genesis 2 & 3) with its punishing God and its grim message of disobedience, sin, guilt, suffering and the banishment of Adam and Eve from the Garden of Eden. They demoted the Queen of Heaven—whose title

was 'Mother of All Living'—into the human figure of Eve, giving her the same title as the former Goddess and placing two Trees in the Garden of Eden instead of one. They blamed Eve for the sin of disobedience that brought about the Fall and for bringing sin, suffering, and death into the world. Henceforth, all women would be contaminated by Eve's sin and would have to be under men's control lest they create further disasters.

Yahweh was left as the sole Creator God: The Divine Feminine aspect of God was deleted from the godhead and from Judaism. The only place where the concept of the sacred marriage of the two aspects of deity survived was in the later mystical Jewish tradition of Kabbalah, known as The Voice of the Dove. The presence of the Divine Feminine in the godhead was not only banished from Judaism, but also from Christianity because it took its image of God from the Old Testament. At the Council of Nicaea in 325 CE, the Trinity was defined in wholly male imagery and the Holy Spirit lost its previous feminine identity."

Margaret Barker writes in her book, *Temple Theology* that "the most important result of Josiah's expunging was the introduction of monotheism."

TO me, it is the rejection of the Divine Feminine part of God, the Holy Spirit, known as the limitless connecting web of life, along with the devaluation of anything associated with the feminine, that has created so much of the chaos we are experiencing in our world. Since our Divine Mother was the connecting web of life, with her rejection came the feeling of separation. We lost our awareness of being one with God, with nature, and all that is!

Reading the Story of Adam and Eve Without the Fall of Man Spin:

If we look at the Adam and Eve story, as it was first added to the Bible and before the later re-interpretation that created the Fall of Man twist, how could this story of Adam and Eve be understood?

Margaret Barker views this parable through the lens of Temple Theology. In her talk, "A Walk Through the Old Testament," she shares the viewpoint that in this story, Adam and Eve were given full access to the Tree of Life, which represented knowledge in the form of Wisdom. However, they disobeyed and instead chose the Tree of Knowledge of Good and Evil, which they were told not to eat from. So, the transgression Adam and Eve committed was in the **type** of knowledge they chose (we can see how this reflects the rejection of the Holy Spirit's Wisdom). Margaret asks how much of our divine nature have we lost because of the type of knowledge, the knowledge not coming from Divine Wisdom, that we have chosen, as individuals and as a humanity? What is running our society? Ironically, we can especially ask, what type of knowledge was chosen when additions and subtractions were made to change the Holy Bible?

Hearing this triggered an epiphany in me, as I started to understand that Jesus came to teach and lead us on a path of transformation by choosing the right kind of knowledge derived from Wisdom. What a healthy, beautiful condition the planet would be in if we made choices coming from that higher knowledge, Wisdom. How this would have improved our priorities. From looking at the current state of the world, regarding how the world is being run and led, we continue to predominantly employ the lower type of knowledge.

The Meaning of Image

Let's look at the word **image** in the original Genesis, where it talks about the beautiful partnership meant for us. Image is translated from the Hebrew word tselem, and it means "form, identity, resemblance, figure." The meaning of the word "image" is easy to visualize. If I were to paint an image of someone or take a photographic image of them—I would have created something resembling that person. God made **them**, man and woman, in his **image**: Father God and Mother Holy Spirit. We, men and women, reflect their image.

Right from the beginning, there are masculine and feminine. That was part of the grand plan. In this original partnership, there is a true sense of mutual love, respect, and equality, that harmoniously benefits each partaker.

If we had kept this understanding of the equal, supportive, and loving companionship meant for us from the beginning, it would have deepened the relationships between men and women. We are part of God, and God is part of us in the same manner, with each gender bringing their complementary, harmonizing gifts to the table.

Ruah Means Feminine Spirit

When examining the Bible, it is necessary to know that the original languages of the texts were Aramaic and Hebrew, with some Greek. The language Jesus himself spoke was Aramaic. Both Aramaic and Hebrew are gendered languages, similar to Spanish or German. For example, in German the vase would be *die* Vase—using the feminine "the" makes the vase also feminine. The ball would be *der* Ball making the ball masculine in nature. In the Biblical languages of Aramaic and Hebrew, the word for Spirit is Ruah, and Ruah is a feminine word, meaning feminine spirit and breath.

When they translated the Bible to Greek, however, the word for spirit was neutral in that language and everything was changed respectively. Not until further down the line, when the Bible was translated into Latin, did they find a language where spirit was a masculine word.

In the English language, there is no gender attached to the word spirit. It would make sense then to go with the gender Jesus used when speaking of the Holy Spirit for our translations, but the translators may not have had access to those translations. Since every word in the Bible has such great implications, the safest bet that we are getting it right is to keep true to Jesus' words. However, it is possible that at the time, the translators only had knowledge of, or access to, the Latin translation. So, they aligned with this translation which changed the gender of our Mother Holy Spirit to the male Spiritus Sanctus. This was likely completely unintentional—though much additional editing was required down the line, as we'll soon see.

The claim that is often made is that the Holy Spirit had been referred to as "she" by Jesus by happenstance because the word spirit *happened* to be feminine in Aramaic. The feminine pronouns didn't actually mean that she was feminine, even when accompanied by feminine verbs. Yet, at the same time, it is acknowledged that she has personhood. If we used the happenstance logic, then speaking to and about our God Holy Spirit as a "she," holds the same significance as putting the feminine "the" in front of an object such as the vase or the blanket, which happens to be feminine in some languages. The Holy Spirit is not an inanimate object, where interchanging gender according to language has no consequence. The Holy Spirit is God! Jesus would not have thoughtlessly called **someone** with personhood, especially someone as significant as the Holy Spirit, "she" if she was in fact a "he" or a genderless spirit. When speaking of the Holy Spirit, he is not talking about the word spirit *generically*. Jesus is referring to a **distinct spirit**—the Holy Spirit. He called the Holy Spirit "she" because she is female.

The Fluid, Multi-Layered Aramaic and Hebrew Languages

Much of our misunderstanding of the Bible was created by inaccurate translations. Exploring the complexity of the poetic, allegorical, fluid, ancient Aramaic, and Hebrew languages helps shed light on what may have happened. These languages are unlike our exceedingly literal English, making them difficult to translate accurately. This also gives a translator a little room for his lens of perception to affect his translations, even if unconsciously. With more women scholars learning the ancient Aramaic language, more discrepancies in translation and punctuation have been noticed. Both Aramaic and Hebrew are languages with multiple layers of meaning, with multiple choices, and in their fluidity, they are written without punctuation. You can conceive how challenging it would be to find the meaning and then find a way of expressing it in our language.

Imagine how simply adding the punctuation alone can change the feeling and meaning of what is being conveyed. We've all seen funny examples of misplaced or omitted commas posted online. "Let's eat, grandma." says something entirely different than "Let's eat grandma. Or—this one, which is an especially appropriate example of what can be done. "Woman: without her, man is nothing." versus "Woman without her man is nothing." You can see how punctuation choices can utterly change meaning. Again, translation choices were made that left women on the short end of the stick when we scrutinize what the original texts actually said.

All of the gospels, whether written in Aramaic, Hebrew or Greek were not safe from word changes. Elizabeth A.

McCabe identified and recorded proof of gender bias in the Greek to English translations. For example, she found the meaning of Greek words that made it clear women held positions of leadership and authority, altered. Words such as diakonos and prostatis, meant deacon and leader, as well as servant. For example, a minister is the servant to God and the people, but as a minister he is also the church leader. This word was translated to leader when describing the men in their positions. But the same words used for women in the same situations were translated to servant in most English translations, including the King James version. It's also said that the words used for proclaiming that men should rule over women are better translated to say that men should care for women. You can see what a seriously distorted picture changing these words creates.

215 Manuscripts Depicting a Female Holy Spirit

It was exciting to come across the brilliant book, *Finding Holy Spirit Mother*, where Ally Kateusz dispels with the claim that in some cases Ruah can be masculine in relation to the Holy Spirit. Kateusz references a book, *The Meaning of Ruah at Qumran*, in which the author, Arthur Everett Sekki, did an extensive study of 215 manuscripts that were part of the Dead Sea Scrolls, with a focus on the ancient theology around the Holy Spirit. The manuscripts were written in Hebrew and Aramaic and Ally Kateusz says that they were used during Jesus' time! It is significant that these texts were used during the time that Jesus lived!

As mentioned before, since Aramaic and Hebrew are fluid languages, words can have multiple meanings, depending on how they are used and for whom. Arthur Everett Sekki revealed in this dissertation, after examining one manuscript after the other, looking to see what gender was being used when the Holy Spirit was being talked about, vs when talking about the spirit of the people, or when talking about something quite opposite, a demonic spirit. Sure enough, the gender changed according to use! What Arthur Everett Sekki found was that the pronouns for Ruah were almost always changed to masculine when used for the spirit of Belial, a Demon. But whenever Ruah was used for the spirit of the people and for the Spirit of God, the Holy Spirit, Ruah was used in its feminine form! Which proves that using the female gender for the Holy Spirit is not random, but intentional and important!

People will say that God is androgynous, all genders— but then strip the trinity of all female beings. Telling women that we can just "know it inside" that God is both male and female, while presenting an all-male God to the outside world, won't do.

Though some gender changes were likely accidental during translation from other languages, it is difficult to believe it continued to be completely inadvertent when so much more editing would need to have taken place to make those changes, which included the removal of words, such as "Mother". And it doesn't stop there. Additionally, there is evidence showing that the status of women in the Bible, including women in leadership roles, were diminished through editing long after the Bible was written, which we will explore later.

With the gender of the Holy Spirit changed, women and girls are deprived of their representation in God. What has been taken from them is the sense of being connected to and part of God in the same way men are. Eliminating any reflection of women or the feminine in God, has also dangerously and wrongly diminished women and girl's value in the eyes of men and impacted their place in the world and how they are treated. From lost opportunities simply never allowed to them, to infanticide, human trafficking and murder, and so much more—there's been an unquestionable impact.

This deletion of our Divine Mother has also made anything associated with the feminine somehow less than, from our emotions to Mother Nature, which are associated with the feminine. Boys and men have been ridiculed for showing emotions in a healthy manner because crying or having all those feelings, is seen as feminine. Not allowing men to openly feel and work through their emotions is devastating to their mental health. For example, the suicide rate for men has been higher than for women. Men are also more likely to act out in violence. Everything there is and everyone who is has pieces of the feminine in themselves to varying degrees, depending on gender and orientation. Therefore, debasing the feminine has hurt everyone and everything.

As we move through the Old Testament, as well as the New Testament, we will continue to see the clues where the radiant presence of our Mother Holy Spirit and her image were weeded out. She had such a great presence in the Bible before, and just enough evidence of her remains for us to see that she was there and for us to understand the importance of her return.

Names for Holy Spirit

The Holy Spirit has been given many names. Connecting to those names makes it easier for us to connect to her. To start our journey and to help recognize her in texts, it's helpful to share a few of them. Just as in writings, we see a variety of names for God the Father and the same goes for the Holy Spirit. Here are a few examples, though not exhaustive.

Father God
God, Father God, Lord, Abba, Divine Father, HaShem, Allah, God Almighty, Jehovah, Yahweh

Holy Spirit
Holy Spirit, Shekinah, Asherah, Wisdom, Mother God, Divine Mother, Sophia, Spirit of Truth, Queen of Heaven, Queen of the Angels, Holy Ghost, Yahweh

The Shekinah

One of the names I've mentioned for the Holy Spirit is the Shekinah, the Divine Feminine aspect of God in Jewish mysticism. Shekinah means dwelling, divine presence, the manifestation of God here on earth, God's glory, an indwelling Bride. Shekinah is Wisdom. She is the connecting web of life, the soul of the cosmos, the intermediary between the unknowable and life here on earth. The Shekinah, sadly, like the Holy Spirit, has also gone through a gender transformation over time. But considerably more of her story can still be found, though not within traditional Judaism but if you look within their mystical tradition of Kabbalah. To me, much indicates that the Holy Spirit and Shekinah are the same person, though there may appear to be a slight variation in the roles and attributes, as both were viewed through the lens of each tradition. The strong similarities and identities can't be ignored.

In *The Dream of the Cosmos*, Anne Baring gives a wonderful description of the Shekinah of Kabbalah, drawing on the work of the great scholar Gershom Scholem. Kabbalah was the mystical tradition of Judaism, known as the Voice of the Dove and The Jewels of the Heavenly Bride. Anne Baring has graciously shared her wisdom with us here.

> The Shekinah is the image of the Divine
> Feminine or the Feminine Face of God as
> it was conceived in this mystical tradition
> of Judaism. In the imagery and cosmology
> of the Shekinah, we encounter the most
> complete description of Divine Wisdom and
> the Holy Spirit as well as the indissoluble

relationship between the two primary
aspects of the god-head that have been lost
or hidden for centuries.

The Shekinah is the Voice or Word of God,
the Wisdom of God, the Glory of God, the
Compassion of God, the Active Presence
of God: intermediary between the mystery
of the unknowable source or ground and
this world of its ultimate manifestation.
The concept of the Shekinah as Divine
Wisdom and Holy Spirit offers one of the
most incandescent, vivid and powerful
images of the immanence of the divine in
this dimension. It transmutes all creation,
including the apparent insignificance and
ordinariness of everyday life, into something
to be loved, embraced, honoured and
celebrated because it is the epiphany or
shining forth of the divine intelligence and
love that has brought it into being and dwells
hidden within it.

The Shekinah, named as Divine Wisdom
and the Holy Spirit – divinity present and
active in the world – supplies the missing
imagery of divine immanence which has
been lost in Judaism, Christianity and Islam.
And this mystical tradition brings together
heaven and earth, the divine and the human,

in a coherent and seamless vision of their essential relationship.

The Shekinah is defined as the feminine aspect of the godhead, as Mother, Beloved, Sister and Bride—imagery that has also been lost in these religions. If recovered and honoured, it could transform our image of God and Nature, not to mention ourselves. The Shekinah gives woman what she has lacked throughout the last two thousand years in western civilization — a sacred image of the Divine Feminine that is reflected at the human level in herself. The Shekinah is Divine Motherhood, named as 'Mother of All Living' — the title that once belonged to the Queen of Heaven in the First Temple and that the Deuteronomists bestowed on Eve in the Myth of the Fall. The ancient tradition of the Divine Feminine, Divine Wisdom and the Holy Spirit, lost in 623 BCE, somehow survived in Kabbalism.

Wisdom of Solomon

Now let's gaze upon the beautiful scripture from the Wisdom of Solomon. I am swept away by this work, generally dated to the mid-first century BC. It is included in the canonical texts in the Catholic Bible but, to our great loss, not in the Protestant Bible. However, it is usually included in the Apocrypha for the Protestants. Since I was raised Lutheran, I missed out on these texts until recently. I'm grateful to have encountered them. It's impossible to read these words without being deeply moved. King Solomon has such a high reverence for the Holy Spirit, aka Wisdom. The quotes are extremely revealing of her nature and gender. They also show that she is one and the same with God, for when God was called upon she came.

Wisdom of Solomon 7:7-10, 12

> ... I called upon God, and the spirit of
> wisdom came upon me: And I preferred her
> before kingdoms and thrones, and esteemed
> riches nothing in comparison of her. Neither
> did I compare unto her any precious stone:
> for all gold in comparison to her, is as little
> as sand, and silver in respect to her shall be
> counted as clay. I loved her above health and
> beauty, and chose to have her instead of light:
> for her light cannot be put out. And I rejoiced
> in all these: for this wisdom went before me,
> and I knew not that she was the Mother of
> them all.

The Holy Spirit as Lady Wisdom

As noted, what made this book necessary is the extensive editing of our Bible, which includes changing the gender of our Mother the Holy Spirit. So, it is interesting that the gender of the Holy Spirit as Wisdom was not changed. This may be because they hoped that we wouldn't connect the dots that they are the same person, and because they came up with the argument that Wisdom, or as she is sometimes called, Lady Wisdom, is not a person, but rather a personification—meaning an attribution. Once they did that, they could then easily make that attribution a part of someone else of their choosing. However, there is clear evidence in Proverbs that we are not talking about an attribution, but rather an individual—Wisdom is a person.

Many of our translations are lacking due to the limits of the English language and the complexities of Hebrew and Aramaic. Numerous meanings are lost, and words can be misunderstood or inaccurately translated, which can cause a person to misinterpret or morph an entire passage into something unintended. But now, more women scholars have learned ancient Aramaic and are able to read and translate the ancient texts. It has been discovered that some early translations appear quite skewed—and to no surprise, not in favor of women.

To be fair, when trying to understand history we always want to keep in mind that there is a need to look through the lens of perception of that culture during that time. If we had been born then, we would have been under the same influence. What was the framework which they saw everything through? Some of the skewed translations simply came from a distorted lens, while other translations were

more likely skewed intentionally to suppress women and their power.

People from only 100 years ago didn't see things the same way we do now. Most certainly there was a completely different perspective over 2,000 years ago. I will repeat this occasionally—we need to keep in mind that the Bible was written during an extremely patriarchal period. This affects the framework through which everything is viewed, perceived, and justified by the scribes when translating or editing text. Society is still under a patriarchal influence today, though things have slowly been changing and healing towards more balance. We are not there yet though. We haven't reached a healthy equilibrium, and our slant on God most certainly has had a hand in this.

As far as what is written in Proverbs goes, some confusion can be understood because there are various parts that genuinely do sound like we are talking about a personification in the translated to English version. However, as many scholars have pointed out, when you read Proverbs mindfully, even with all of the redactions, it becomes evident that we are talking about a person.

There are clear clues that Wisdom is not a personification—she is a Spirit (the Holy Spirit). She even calls herself a Spirit in Proverbs. I share a text that I understand to be Wisdom's response to her rejection after her expulsion from the temple, which makes it even more clear that we are talking about what happened to the Holy Spirit here.

Proverbs 1:20-24

> Wisdom preacheth abroad, she uttereth
> **her voice** in the streets:
> At the head of multitudes she crieth out,
> in the entrances of the gates of the city she

uttereth her words, saying, O children,
how long will you love childishness, and
fools covet those things that are hurtful
to themselves, and the unwise hate
knowledge? Turn ye at my reproof: behold
I will utter **my spirit** to you, and will shew
you my words. Because I called, and you
refused: **I have stretched out my hand**,
and there was none that regarded.

She says, "Behold I will utter my spirit unto you," which makes it clear that we are talking about someone with personhood. A personification doesn't possess a spirit. The word **spirit** is a critical word here, because it makes it apparent that we are talking about Wisdom as a someone who pours her spirit into us. By the way, this is what the Holy Spirit is known to do!

Yet, some contemporary versions of the Bible removed the word "spirit" and changed it to "thought." From spirit to thought is a big leap for me, because the word spirit was a big clue that "she" is a being. In this case, however, the word "thought" still gives us a strong indication as well, because for someone to have thoughts, they must have personhood.

Also, it says that Wisdom reached out her hand, not something an attribute has. Then Exodus, quoted here from the 1899 Douay-Rheims Bible, links the Holy Spirit with Wisdom further.

Exodus 28:3

And thou shalt speak to all the wise of heart,
whom I have filled with the spirit of wisdom

On her website, Deidre Havrelock points out another connection between Wisdom and the Holy Spirit in this verse, which I had missed: the stretching out of Wisdom's hands. Deidre Havrelock shares that not only can Wisdom be poured or dwell in us, but she can be passed on by the laying of hands, which is how the Apostles filled believers with the Holy Spirit!

Acts 8:17

> Then they laid their hands on them, and they
> received the Holy Ghost.

The recognition of the Holy Spirit/Holy Ghost being the same person as Wisdom is not new. Theophilus of Antioch, the 7th Bishop of Antioch (c. 169–c. 183) and Irenaeus, a Greek Bishop declared that the Holy Spirit is Wisdom!

We've discussed the Holy Spirit as being the intermediary between the Mystery of the Unknowable Source and this world. She is the Active Presence of God. It is extraordinary that other religions reflect similar knowledge. For we all have the same God, we just have given Him/Her different names and interpret teachings differently, albeit with so many common threads. For example, one of many Hindu denominations, Shaktism, has the Goddess Shakti as a powerful female creating force. She is considered to be the active aspect of the godhead and is looked upon as the primordial energy of the cosmos. Do you see the shared knowledge and understanding?

It's important to appreciate that since the beginning of time, Wisdom was associated with the Goddess. We already mentioned Asherah. In Greek mythology, the virgin goddess Athena was also always associated with Wisdom—different names were given to the Holy Spirit depending on time, place, culture, and perception. But Wisdom was identified as a person, a female person—not just an essence—Wisdom was known as the personified, divine female Spirit of God.

~.~.~.~.~

Beyond Proverbs, there are plenty more confirmations of the feminine face of God in other writings and gospels not included in our canonical texts. I do hope you take the time to read some of them. They can stimulate an opening of our consciousness when we recognize that they are talking about a Mother God and her profound presence and meaning in our lives.

Meanwhile, let's look at Sirach (aka Ecclesiasticus) in the Old Testament next.

More Proof in Sirach

Sirach (Ecclesiasticus) has some of the most powerful verses in the Bible when it comes to speaking of what is happening right now on our planet. They prophesy about what was done to Wisdom, the Holy Spirit, and its impact us. Please take your time and read these words thoughtfully. Our Mother is warning us how vital it is to get to know her, to adhere to and learn from her.

Sirach 6: 21-23, 27-32

> How very unpleasant is wisdom to the
> unlearned, and the unwise will not continue
> with her. She shall be to them as a mighty
> stone of trial, and they will cast her from
> them before long. For the wisdom of doctrine
> is according to her name, and she is not
> manifest unto many, but with them to whom
> she is known, she continueth even to the
> sight of God. Come to her with all thy mind,
> and keep her ways with all thy power. Search
> for her, and she shall be made known to thee,
> and when thou hast gotten her, let her not go.
> For in the latter end thy shall find rest in her,
> and she shall be turned into thy joy. Then
> shall her fetters be a strong defence for thee,
> and a firm foundation, and her chain a robe
> of glory: For in her is the beauty of life...

Notice the similarities when Sirach speaks of Lady Wisdom's robe of glory, and the Shekinah is known as Shekinah Glory. It also speaks of how we can become filled with Wisdom, especially while praying—which is what the

Holy Spirit is known for. Let's continue, as we will see that Wisdom was also called Mother and Wife.

Sirach 15: 2-3, 5-8

> And she will meet him [them] as an honourable **mother**, and will receive him [them] as a wife married of a virgin.
> And in the midst of the church she shall open his [their] mouth[s], and shall fill him [them] with the spirit of wisdom and understanding, and shall clothe him [them] with a robe of glory. She shall heap upon him [them] a treasure of joy and gladness, and shall cause him [them] to inherit an everlasting name. But foolish men [and women] shall not obtain her, and wise men [and women] shall meet her, foolish men [and women] shall not see her: for she is far from pride and deceit. Lying men [and women] shall not be mindful of her: but men [and women] that speak truth shall be found with her, and shall advance, even till they come to the sight of God.

The New Testament

Now we get to the New Testament. The New Testament speaks of the new covenant explained in the life and death of Jesus. It is interesting to know that after Jesus was crucified, there was no common consensus among the Christians as to what his message was and what Christianity should look like. There were debates and varying views—even amongst his followers—as to what the true meaning of Jesus' teachings was.

Jesus taught orally. Nothing had been documented in writing while he was teaching and the gospels we have come to know were not written down until two generations after his crucifixion. However, a new gospel has come to light that we will talk about later. Meanwhile, think about that—that's a long time after. We have all experienced reminiscing with a friend or family member about an event we both partook in, and each of us tends to recall and cognize the details a bit differently—which accounts for the variances. We also want to note that the New Testament has unfortunately gone through edits along the way.

Originally, we had considerably more gospels to learn from and to get a sense of Jesus' life and teachings. Some gospels were written in different time periods and under different philosophical influences.

Though Jesus included women as disciples and apostles, and his respect for them was feministic in nature, each gospel author filtered Jesus' teaching through their extremely patriarchal lens and their capacity to understand his message, during those times. Realizing this is important. For example, Mary Magdalene was the disciple who was said to understand Jesus' teachings the most completely, which drew much jealousy in her direction. The Gospel of Mary, which would not have been patriarchal in nature, was among those commanded to be destroyed. But fragments of this significant Gospel were discovered in 1896 in a fifth-century papyrus codex written in Sahidic Coptic, along with other writings. Two more fragments of this Gospel were found that were written in Greek.

Originally, the large collection of gospels that existed were not given the labels of canonical or Gnostic. They were all simply one of the many gospels. Some common beliefs ran through most of them, along with small and rather large differences. I imagine it was similar to what we have today with our diversity of Christian faiths, such as Baptist, Lutheran, Christian Science, Evangelical, Catholic, and so on. Only, it probably was more scattered and chaotic back then. If we look at the political climate, it was a more violent and chaotic society.

The early Church Fathers likely decided it was necessary to create a unified belief system, using the Gospels with the most common threads running through them and whatever else they felt was important for church building, to give society and the Christian faith strength and structure. The Christian canon was approved by various councils and popes. So, it seems that it was not all about exacting control in the darkest sense, for many involved at that time.

Irenaeus was a Greek Bishop who took part in the development of Christian theology. He stood firmly against Gnosticism, but both he and Theophilus of Antioch linked our Mother Holy Spirit with the feminine Wisdom! This is probably one of the reasons why she was recognized, and we can find evidence of her, in most of the earliest gospels.

Others went hard to work later to remove her, and these acts have more of an ulterior motive air to them.

What stands out in all gospels, when looking at the original message Jesus intended is that Jesus taught a heart-centered spirituality, which honored both the masculine and the feminine—men and women. Jesus included women in his ministry, which was unusual at that time.

It's important to consciously acknowledge within ourselves that we will not give the redactors the power to diminish what is written in the Bible or take away our reverence for it. Realizing that the Bible was redacted by scribes has exasperated and infuriated many, me included, but it has never diminished the preciousness of the Bible in my eyes, knowing all it still contains. We are not alone in our exasperation. Jesus himself had strong words for the scribes and Pharisees calling them "hypocrites" and "blind guides", among other things, in Matthew 23. It is some of their undertakings I mistrust. But if we educate ourselves, we can see our way around some of what they have done.

The New Testament is ripe with wisdom, and we are lucky to have found some of the gospels meant to be destroyed. Making comparisons and looking for commonalities among the gospels will help us get a closer sense of what some of the redactions to the original canonical texts likely were.

In the next pages, I share scholarly discoveries and varying opinions regarding some of the stories in the New Testament. First, we'll start at the beginning of Jesus's life with the conception story.

Matthew 23: 25-28

Woe to you scribes and Pharisees,
hypocrites; because you make clean the
outside of a cup and of the dish, but within
you are full of rapine and uncleanliness.
Thou blind Pharisee, first make clean the
inside of the cup and of the dish, that the
outside may become clean. Woe to you
scribes and Pharisees, hypocrites; because
you are like the whited sepulchres, which
outwardly appear to men beautiful, but
within are full of dead men's bones, and of
all filthiness. So you also outwardly indeed
appear to men just; but inwardly you are full
of hypocrisy and iniquity.

The Story of Jesus's Conception

Opening with the story of how Jesus was conceived in the New Testament, we see there can be issues simply in clearly deciphering what we are reading. This is understandable as the story is beautiful, though sometimes confusing with challenging wording. I came across an article, "The Blasphemy of Saint Augustine" written by lawyer, James Hale, where he painstakingly examined what took place. As a legal eagle, he is a pro at scrutinizing what a statement precisely conveys. He tells us to look at the Annunciation where the Angel Gabriel announces to Mary that she has been chosen to be the one to give birth to the Messiah. We can find this in Luke:

Luke 1: 31-36

> Behold thy shall conceive in thy womb, and shalt bring forth a son; and though shalt call his name Jesus. He shall be great, and shall be called the Son of the Most High; and the Lord God shall give unto him the throne of David his father; and he shall reign in the house of Jacob for ever. And of his kingdom there shall be no end. And Mary said to the angel: How shall this be done, because I know not man? And the angel answering, said to her: The Holy Ghost shall come upon thee, and the power of the most High shall overshadow thee
> And therefore also the Holy which shall be born of thee shall be called the Son of God.

Hale explains that the usual way people have interpreted this passage is that Jesus was conceived through a mystical union *exclusively* between Mary and the Holy Spirit. But this is not at all what it says. James Hale kindly allowed me to include that excerpt from his article here:

> "... a closer look at the process by which Jesus was conceived, as described by Gabriel, clearly involves two separate steps and, more importantly, two separate persons of the Trinity, not just one:
>
> The Holy Ghost shall come upon thee, **and** the power of the Highest shall overshadow thee: therefore also that holy...which shall be born of thee shall be called the Son of God.
>
> **In step one**, the Holy Spirit will "come upon" Mary. **Then, and only then**, will the "power of the Highest" overshadow her. How else can we make sense of this than by seeing it as the supernatural union, not just between Mary and the Holy Spirit, but involving the 'Highest' as well?
>
> You need not look very far to determine precisely who Gabriel meant by the 'Highest'. First, we can see from the immediate context that the 'Highest' is distinct from the 'Holy Ghost'. Second, in a previous verse, Gabriel says to Mary that the son she will bear and

name Jesus will be "called the Son of the Highest."

Clearly, then, Gabriel has the Father in mind when he refers to the 'Highest.' Thus, what is being pictured here is **a union, first and foremost, between the Father and the Holy Spirit**, as eternal Spouse of the Father and eternal Mother of the Son. Mary's involvement in this union is secondary (**"therefore also"**), limited to the **role of the human vessel** who will bear and give birth to the incarnate Son of God. She serves as Christ's temporal mother, and in, this she is "blessed among women," but it would be quite impossible for her to be the "Mother of God" in any way other than this temporal sense.

–James Hale

This was a big "ah-ha" moment for me. It made sense. The Divine Father and the Divine Mother came **together** to birth the Divine child. Birth requires a father and mother, and then Mary received the highest honor among women of being the one chosen to give physical birth to the Divine Son as his earthly mother.

In the Gospel of Philip, Philip chastises those who believed that Mary would have been physically impregnated by the Holy Spirit alone. In verse 14, he responds exasperated that some are saying that Mary conceived by the Holy Spirit, emphatically stating that they are wrong! He asks when did a woman ever get pregnant by another woman? It is apparent that during the time Philip lived, the Holy Spirit was primarily known as being female.

To further complicate things, for the longest time when I heard about the immaculate conception story, I imagined it was referring to Jesus having been immaculately conceived. But the Immaculate Conception story is not about Jesus' conception. Instead, it refers to the conception of his mother, Mary! You see, Augustine of Hippo's declaration that we are all born with original sin and that the act of sex itself is sinful; a declaration that so many theologians disputed even at that time, complicated things, because this is not what it said originally in the Bible about us, and (big sigh of relief) it is not what Jesus taught. With their new original sin declaration, the church needed to find an explanation as to how Jesus could enter this world through a tarnished human being. They decided that Mother Mary must have been immaculately conceived. This story about Mary herself being immaculately conceived can also not be found in the Bible. The story was introduced in 1854 by Pope Pius IX.

This information was new to me. Now, what James Hale points out makes even more sense. The dilemma that Mary had to have been immaculately conceived comes from interpreting the story to say that Jesus was conceived between the union of Mary, a woman, and the Holy Spirit, rather than that Jesus was conceived through a pure Holy Union between Father God and Mother God and then Mary was given the most incredible, highest-honor of being the one to give birth to the Divine Son. This honor is extraordinary beyond words, but she would not need to be immaculately conceived in this scenario. It would be fine if she had more children along the way as well.

When I was younger, I didn't know that Jesus had siblings. Some still claim that he did not, but it talks about them right there in the Bible in several places, including in Matthew.

Matthew 13:55-56

> Is this not the carpenter's son? Is not his
> mother called Mary, and his brethren James,
> and Joseph, and Simon, and Jude: And his
> sisters, are they not with us?

The new insights above helped me to imagine Jesus' life more fully and resulted in me feeling even closer in heart to him, to Mother Mary, and to God. I hope the more you discover and explore, the closer your relationship with them becomes as well.

We can imagine some of the debates amongst Christians now. Not all Christian denominations accepted the immaculate conception story. Everyone is doing their best with what we know. It's good to be aware of different views and details, and they should not be the cause of division! It's Jesus' core teachings that are most important and they are about our sisterhood and brotherhood. Love one another, with our differences and all.

To be a Father is Relational

Apart from the immaculate conception story, James Hale points out something else in his article that has been staring us all in the face. God is called our Father. The word father is relational! You can't be considered a father without a mother and a child. You can be a guy, a man, a doctor, a soccer player, or whatever. But to be given the title of "father", you must have a child. To give birth to a child, there needs to be a mother. The first relationship for a male who will father a child is with the woman who will be the mother. To be God the Father to a Divine Child, there must be a God the Mother.

Hale points out that, yes, there can be a completely abstract use of the word, such as George Washington as the father of our country. But there is nothing remotely abstract about Jesus' loving relationship with his father. It is an intimate, meaningful father-son relationship.

Hale also posits that when we acknowledge Jesus as being divine, then that must mean that the eternal Son pre-existed the incarnate Christ. He didn't just come into being the moment he was born of Mary. He incarnated at the time through physical birth here on earth. However, he has always existed, even before that, as part of God, in what we now see as a Holy Trinity, along with the Father and the Mother.

Jesus Called the Holy Spirit Mother

We discussed earlier that Jesus would not have haphazardly called the Holy Spirit "she" if it was not a woman. Did you know that we have proof he also specifically called her Mother?

Jesus clarifies the truth about the Holy Spirit's gender through his own words right after his baptism. We never would have known about this saying if others hadn't studied and recorded it, because, like the many other gospels, it was destroyed. But luckily what Jesus was quoted saying in that Gospel was written down by Bishop Papias, who, according to St. Irenaeus, knew Apostle John. Papias mentioned that Matthew himself had written a Gospel using his native Hebrew! This is sometimes called the Authentic Gospel of Matthew since this is a rare first-person account, however, it is best known as the Gospel of the Hebrews.

How precious to us to finally have a Gospel that is a first-person account! One would think this Gospel especially would have been protected and treasured! Instead, it was destroyed, and no copy of it survived. Why would they do such a thing to a first-person account by Matthew!? Matthew is a recognized disciple and apostle! Could it be because of something the Gospel contained? We are at least blessed then that, despite this attempted erasure, it came to our knowledge along with at least one of its quotes, because besides Bishop Papias, early Christian Theologians such as Clement of Alexandria, Origen, and several others wrote about it! Because of these writings, this illuminating Gospel did not completely disappear from our awareness.

According to the Authentic Gospel of Matthew, also known as the Gospel of the Hebrews, right after Jesus' baptism when the Holy Spirit descends on Jesus like a dove and exclaims that Jesus is her beloved son, Jesus is quoted as saying about her, "Even so did my Mother, the Holy Spirit, take me..." There we have it! "Even so did my Mother, the Holy Spirit..." Jesus himself not only called the Holy Spirit she, **he called her—Mother**!

How can there be any question? Matthew makes it clear. We can rejoice in our hearts that all of us have a Divine Mother! We are children of a Father and Mother God.

A fresco painting on the ceiling of the St.Jakobus Church in Urschalling, Bavaria, Germany, built at the end of the 11ᵗʰ century, shows our Mother Holy Spirit between her Divine Husband and Divine Child, in her glorious womanly form. When the church was being renovated, these old frescos were discovered under thick, white paint.

The Holy Trinity:
Missing Our Holy Spirit Mother

Most of us can relate whether we are male or female, that our human mother tends to be the most influential person in our lives growing up. When they removed our Divine Mother from our consciousness, we lost much of the heart and soul of the cosmos, along with her much needed guidance. When I became aware of our Mother Holy Spirit, everything fell naturally into place and felt clearer to me—the Holy Trinity, my relationship with God, and the joy that truly equal relationships would bring on this beautiful journey we call Life. It also helped me to better grasp the fullness of the Divine—the fullness of God. We always have loved Father God and now we have a Mother.

If we look back at what came before Christianity, there is a history to the Trinity. As Christians, we are often told not to look back to this time. Before Christianity, people were heathens or terrible sinners. But that's not true, there were brilliant people and lovely societies, and much like us, they were trying to understand God. The history of civilization begins long before Christianity, or any type of recorded history. As a matter of fact, there is archaeological evidence that a goddess culture had prominence during the pre-historical period. It's important not to close our eyes to what came before because God didn't change once Christianity started. God was God and was always present. Therefore, there are clues and wisdom to be found when we look at what the previous civilizations perceived.

One word that seems derogatory when used by Christians is the word Pagan. So, it was surprising to me the gentle culture I discovered when I read about that belief. I loved that there was often an ecological and nature focus to their practice. Similar to us having different denominations of Christianity, there were different groups of Pagans. But it is exciting and interesting to learn that a large percentage of the Pagans believed, and many still do to this day, in a triune God. There were other cultures that worshiped a triune God as well. But the father, mother, and child triads were very common within the Pagan religion. This was thought to have been absorbed into Christianity, since our relationship with God didn't change, just because some of us became Christians—at least not at first. Then the editing in the Bible started taking place, tampering with that long held wisdom.

Through raised awareness, we can partner God's male and female once again, filling the gaping hole that was created in the abandonment of her, our Mother. Healing God's Image increases opportunities for creating more mutually nurturing relationships for us here on earth. Our appreciation of our human kindredness is enhanced. In the Holy Trinity, our Godly Family reflects our earthly family! We were made in their image.

I have delighted in reading Reverend Dr. Craig Atwood's articles on Moravian Theology, which to me is not that far off from the Lutheran Theology I was raised with. Apparently, Count Zinzendorf had the courage to point out that when it comes to the Holy Trinity—there needs to be a Mother! According to Atwood, around the 1750s Zinzendorf, who was bishop of the Moravian Church, brought the Mother back to the Trinity! The way he wrote about her is deeply heartfelt and moving. Atwood says, "...that devotion to the Holy Spirit as mother was a central part of the church's worship, doctrine, and private devotion for nearly 20 years."

This devotion wasn't only due to the Holy Spirit having been recognized as the Mother in the past, but especially due to Zinzendorf's own deep inner knowing. He preached entire sermons about her, and she was celebrated in the hymns they sang in church!

Sadly, after Zinzendorf died, some of the church elders decided this language around the Holy Spirit's Motherhood needed to be repressed. They wanted to get in line with the other churches. They felt it would benefit them to conform. Many members opposed this, but the repressors won. Records were destroyed and Zinzendorf's writings were purposefully allowed to go out of print. Once again, our Divine Mother was erased and abandoned.

The Lord's Prayer

Think of the impact what we pray every day has on us. When I was quite young, I remember briefly wondering where Mother God was. But my mother taught me the words to the Lord's Prayer, which I was told Jesus himself had given us. The Lord's Prayer begins with "Our Father who art in heaven..." and goes on without the mention of a Mother. Surely if there was a Mother, Jesus would have mentioned her here. For me, the Lord's Prayer helped solidify my strictly male image of God. Since I can remember I have been praying the Lord's Prayer at night.

I can't even describe my ecstatic surprise when I read the more thoughtful translation of that significant prayer brought to light in the book, *Prayers of the Cosmos,* by Neil Douglas-Klotz, where he painstakingly translates every word properly from Aramaic, finding its true meaning in context with the other words. Remember I mentioned the layers of meaning to words in the original language? Douglas-Klotz shares multiple possibilities for the faithful meanings, line for line, for the entire prayer. He gives us a few slightly varying interpretations to take in. He explains the process of finding the emotional, intellectual, and spiritual meaning of each chosen word, explaining his choices—and with this, he lifts a veil.

The original text in this prayer does not open with what we have grown accustomed to. According to Neil Douglas-Klotz, the first more accurate translation choice he gives us for the very first line in what we know as the Lord's Prayer—rather than it saying, "Our Father who art in heaven"—it says, "O Birther! Father-Mother of the Cosmos..."

Read that again. The rest of the prayer continues to be moving and beautiful. What a difference an accurate translation of what Jesus gave us would have made in our lives. I sat there staring at those words, filling my heart with them. I hope everyone exposes themselves to these translations. All this time, we could have been praying to our loving Father God and our loving Mother God—our Divine Parents! Think of the power the ancient translators had to shape our world, our perception of God, by the words they chose to use—and by the words they chose to not to use. How different our views on gender and on life would have been if our nightly prayer had included our Mother. What a difference it would have made if as children all of us would have known God this way!

The rest of the versions for that opening line are genderless, using names for God such as Radiant One. Not one of any of these meticulously rendered interpretations translates to praying to a Father God alone.

The rest of the Lord's Prayer, or God's Prayer, is incredibly soulful and different than what we were told and therefore can take time to get used to. At first, these translations may feel foreign to us, because it is natural to feel more comfortable with the familiar. So first, I only changed the opening of this Prayer for myself. "O Birther! Father-Mother of the Cosmos, hallowed be they names..." With the more accurate translation, there were choices. Soon, the beauty of the original words drew me in. I found the translation that resonated most inside of me. Along with always including a prayer in my own words, I now joyfully pray to our Divine Parents, using the words Jesus gave us every night, feeling a connection to the wholeness of God and the cosmos as never before. My soul rejoices for knowing these words.

The Holy Spirit as a Dove

At Jesus' baptism, the Holy Spirit is described as descending like a dove. Being "***like a*** dove" is not the same as "being a dove." Yet painting after painting, this is how we see the Holy Spirit depicted. The Holy Spirit is also described as having the voice of a dove, which means her voice is beautifully lyrical, surpassing any human voice in its beauty. It's allegorical. It doesn't mean she sounds like a bird.

Even with the dove as a symbol, a metaphor, for the Holy Spirit, it may be possible that the feminine Holy Spirit at times, chooses to take on the form of a dove as the intermediary here on earth. So, it is lovely having the dove as one of her symbols—others include breath, fire, and olive oil.

I used the dove symbol myself in my children's film and book, *Dorme: A Magical Dreamland Visit*, where a child goes on a dreamland quest to release the Mother Holy Spirit, as the Divine Feminine and Dove of Peace into the world.

There is incredible beauty and meaning in symbolism. The dove symbol is used for the Shekinah as well. The dove symbol is often used to represent peace and love. The problem I realized, in researching for this book is, that we seem to have lost the person in the symbol. So much so, that I found it nearly impossible to find any historical paintings or old works of art celebrating her as the feminine part of God—or anything respectfully depicting her in her female form, the image that we women were made in. We can imagine having this neutral symbol depicting the Holy Spirit in art and form was necessary to keep her genderless or male.

I was therefore elated when I came across the old, 14th-century fresco painting of her in her womanly form, on the

ceiling of the St. Jakobus Church in Bavaria, Germany. The telling image is included in this book a few pages earlier. But that was all I found to be left of the historical images of the Holy Spirit as the woman and mother that she is. Though, there may be one more in plain sight. There is an ongoing argument that the Holy Spirit is the significant feminine figure under God's arm or the one behind him holding onto his forearm, as depicted in the famous Creation of Man (humankind) painting on the ceiling of the Sistine Chapel.

The Holy Spirit is a female being. Rauch, the Aramaic and Hebrew word for Spirit, additionally means wind or breath. So, she is the invisible presence of God here on earth. However, she was also written about as having female form in texts. Most of the proof of this is gone, but not entirely.

In his original research, "The Holy Spirit as Feminine: Early Christian Testimonies and Their Interpretations", Johannes Van Oort writes about Epiphanius, a Bishop and early Church Father. He wrote a book titled *Panarion,* where he shares the Jewish Christian prophet Elxai's experiences and prophetic revelations. There is a line in the book where he writes about the Holy Spirit having stood over Jesus as a "female being"! This recognition is remarkable. I have a link to the paper in the reference section at the back of this book.

I envision the Holy Spirit standing over Jesus in her feminine form and feel her warm presence. Though the dove is a lovely image, for a full appreciation and sense of the Holy Spirit—it is essential that we also at times depict her as the feminine being that she is.

Blasphemy Against the Holy Spirit

As if the scribes working away at editing the Bible weren't enough for us to deal with. Lawyer James Hale calls out Saint Augustine, in his article, "The Blasphemy of Saint Augustine," for his part in later further reinterpreting Biblical text against the presence of a female Holy Spirit. Augustine decided that having called the Holy Spirit Mother and feminine in the past had been 'absurd.' So obviously he acknowledged that she was seen as a woman and a mother.

Augustine, though a brilliant man in many ways, brought with him what we call Augustinian guilt—he beat himself up for having been promiscuous in his past and blamed women for making him feel lustful. He brought his guilt with him and turned Christianity into a religion of guilt and fear. Many wise theologians disagreed with and were concerned about Augustine's darker take on the Adam and Eve story, already back then. It feels as though his spin was chosen over Old Testament wisdom and Jesus's love-based teachings, because building on the mainstays of guilt and fear gave the leaders more control.

In our present times, there may be church leaders who know the truth about the Holy Spirit, but they continue to fight to keep things as they are. But I'd like to believe that when most contemporary preachers and church leaders are speaking, they are simply expounding on what they have always been taught and therefore wholeheartedly believe. So, it becomes a complicated web to untangle. People don't want to let go of a lifetime of belief or teaching, which is understandable. They may fear doing something sacrilegious. But according to James Hale and many leading contemporary theologians, that already happened by the violation against our Mother Holy Spirit, a long time ago. We are trying to rectify this now, for a more authentic relationship with God and a healthier humanity.

When we were stripped of our Divine Mother, her attributes needed to be reallocated. Many of the Holy Spirit's qualities and names were at first transferred and deflected to Eve in the Bible, then to Mother Mary by the patriarchs. Mary was sometimes called the second Eve, though she had remained obedient to God. Mary and Eve were flesh and bone women. Both have profound places in Christianity, Eve as the first woman and Mary as the venerated mother of Jesus, but they weren't God.

Mary is most certainly highly honored and blessed among all women, and she brings us incredible blessings of her own. This will never change. She was chosen to courageously help fulfill God's plan. There is also reason to believe that she was a leader, along with Mary Magdalene, in the Jesus movement. She did not sit on the sidelines. But titles such as, "The Queen of Heaven" or "Queen of the Angels," always belonged to our Mother, the Holy Spirit. They assigned those and other powers of the Holy Spirit over to Mary instead, because she was human. Though she was elevated among other women, she could never have the same power as Mother/God for humanity. What they did was meant to placate us women. Even if we didn't have a Mother God, at least we had Mary. When in reality we are divinely blessed to have *both* Mother God *and* Mother Mary.

It also diverted a lot of our prayers and possibly influenced our understanding regarding some of our spiritual experiences. Even the earlier works on the Divine Feminine in the back of this book, before all this came to light, may have given some of the Holy Spirit's gifts over to others.

Once these brilliant scholars started uncovering what happened, however, they were the first to share it with the world through their newer writings! Theologians and scholars of both genders have become aware of what happened and are speaking up. The veil is thinning and being lifted. People are recognizing that, with what is going on in the world, this is the crucial time for our Great Mother Holy Spirit's return. Later we will discuss what that will mean for the healing of our planet.

Mary will continue to be highly revered for all eternity; she will not be diminished. We can now add to our heart consciousness that there is a Mother God! We can restore her Godly attributes to her. At first, this will require an emotional adjustment. When this is accomplished, women and girls can more fully embrace their selfhood, power, and gifts again. They can contribute more to society, thus helping to lift the feminine energies in a healthy balance with the masculine. This is what makes it vitally necessary that we get more women into leadership positions.

With the feminine also reflected in the God Head, men's and women's relationships can heal and grow closer, allowing them to experience a deeper connection. Humanity can experience a more authentic relationship with all of God's wholeness! If we choose to continue to deny our Mother Holy Spirit, it doesn't change that one day we will all need to answer to her.

Being Born Again Through the Mother Holy Spirit

Considering all that we have discussed thus far, many of us likely find it difficult to believe the Holy Spirit's gender change was entirely inadvertent. Especially when we find further evidence showing that the status of women in general in the Bible, especially women in leadership roles, was altered through redactions long after the Bible was written, which we will look at later. There was just too much editing going on that noticeably changed what took place in a story and what the message was—for all of it to have been accidental. Many changes feel deliberate with a purpose.

The gender change becomes especially awkward when talking about "being born again," considering the simple fact that we were all born of a woman. None of us were born out of a man. With Jesus calling the Spirit of God, "Mother," we can feel confident that giving birth, including rebirth, is the role of our Mother, Holy Spirit.

Professor Gilles Quispel, an esteemed, Dutch theologian and historian of Christianity and Gnosticism, also wrote on this topic after decades of research, exclaiming that we can comprehend that a physical birth requires a mother, so therefore a spiritual rebirth requires a spiritual mother.

After they took the word Mother out of the gospels when referring to being born again, they had to somehow attribute the birthing to the Father, which took some explaining. So, they came up with the justification that it is the *mothering* side of the father that gives birth. A father can be *mothering* all he wants, that is certainly wonderful. But he doesn't give birth. Giving birth is something exclusive to women. When we are born again, we are born through our Divine Mother Holy Spirit.

Here in John, Jesus is asked about how one can be born again and note there is mention of the mother's womb.

John 3:1-5

> And there was a man of the Pharisees, named Nicodemus, a ruler of the Jews. This man came to Jesus by night, and said to him: Rabbi, we know that thou art come a teacher from God; for no man can do these signs which thou dost, unless God be with him. Jesus answered, and said to him: Amen, amen I say to thee, unless a man be born again, he cannot see the kingdom of God. Nicodemus saith to him: How can a man be born when he is old? can he enter a second time into **his mother's womb**, and be born again? Jesus answered: Amen, amen I say to thee, unless a man is born again of water and the Holy Ghost, he cannot enter the kingdom of God.

Mary Magdalene and Women in Leadership

How did Mary Magdalene become the most misrepresented woman in history? Is it possible it had something to do with her standing in Jesus' life, along with her deeper understanding of his teachings, which put her in the position of leadership? Though there's evidence many of the details about her were erased, even with all the editing the Bible went through, we can get a peek at Mary Magdalene's significance. She is still mentioned in the New Testament at least 12 times, which is more than any other woman, besides Jesus' mother Mary.

We are blessed then, that Mary Magdalene has a Gospel of her own. Like the Gospels of Luke or Matthew, there is a Gospel of Mary! This Gospel needed to be hidden so it wouldn't be destroyed along with the other gospels not chosen by the regime at that time. It was found in the Berlin Gnostic Codex discovered in the late-nineteenth century. Sadly, only fragments of her second-century Gospel are left to work with now, due to aging, decomposition, bugs, and so forth.

Many theologians categorize her Gospel as Gnostic. Meggan Watterson however calls it an ascent narrative in her book, *Mary Magdalene Revealed,* because she says that Mary leads us on a path that can liberate our soul during this lifetime. Though the Gospel contains much Gnostic wisdom, it doesn't share a couple of the critical points most Gnostic belief systems have. Watterson says that although the word "ascend" is used, which gives us the feeling of going up, it describes a path of descending deeper inward—into the heart. Anyone on a mystical path will agree that this is what we experience—a going within. Mary is showing

us the Way. In many mystical traditions, it is said that the Divine Feminine leads us to the way of ascension. Imagine what women and men would miss out on if the feminine stayed repressed.

Besides the authenticated Gospel of Mary. There is a second, hidden Gospel of Mary, called The Gospel of the Beloved Companion. This Gospel seems to be another rare first-person account, which I talk about later in this book. What makes it such an incredible treasure is that it has been well preserved, has all the pages intact, and is believed to be written by Mary Magdalene herself!

Yet, in 591 AD, Mary Magdalene the teacher and leader, was suddenly conflated with other women in the Bible named Mary in a Homily by Pope Gregory. From the moment this sermon was delivered, Mary suddenly went from being Jesus' most highly regarded, beloved disciple, who received secret teachings because of her vast capacity to understand, to a penitent sinner and prostitute. Her image got a major makeover. In paintings she was loosely clad, with eyes often looking woefully upward, begging for forgiveness. They took away her identity and with it one of our most powerful role models for girls and women.

The excuse is that Pope Gregory's miscasting of Mary was an accident due to there being many Marys in the Bible—he just got confused. That is possible. It just seems difficult to fathom, with Mary Magdalene having had such a prominent role. Especially since there is reason to believe she was Jesus' wife!

After this miscasting, she was also depicted as a woeful whore, in paintings as well as in literature, theater, films, etc. At last, in the 1960s the Church quietly admitted that an error had been made. Oops, Mary Magdalene had never been a prostitute. But not nearly enough attention was brought to this and for decades after that declaration, Mary Magdalene continues to be inaccurately depicted as the repentant prostitute in church sermons, stories, art, plays, musicals, and films, keeping her misrepresentation alive and engrained in our psyches—even so we now know better!

It would take volumes to share what has been uncovered about Mary's life and her incredible mystical wisdom, but that is not the focus of this book. For brevity, we will stick to a basic introduction. I do recommend reading about Mary Magdalene further. Be selective in your reading though! She has gained much popularity since the movie *The Da Vinci Code* came out—which most recognize as fiction. Since then, a whole slew of books have been written about her. Some are extremely well-researched, but many are far-fetched and mostly fantasy.

Mary Magdalene was believed to have been an educated woman and she had the financial means to help support Jesus' mission. Scholar and author Ann Graham Brock shares how she was the first apostle in her Harvard dissertation and fascinating book, *Mary Magdalene, the First Apostle: A Struggle for Authority*. Karen King is another respected author with an excellent book on Mary Magdalene. Both of these books are meticulously researched and do much to pull out the weeds and raise our awareness as to who she was.

Mary was called, "the woman who knows all." She was Jesus' counterpart and constant companion and stayed present with his mother and his mother's sister at the foot of the cross at his crucifixion when the other disciples fled. She was in the sepulcher garden when the risen Christ appeared to her first, commissioning her to tell the others and spread the news of his resurrection. This is what an apostle would be asked to do, and she had the honor of being the first. This was not happenstance.

Her representation by filmmakers and others so exasperated me, that I produced a no-budget, 30-minute, mixed-genre/docu-film, titled *Who Framed Mary Magdalene?*, which can be found for free on YouTube and Vimeo. The interviews, starting with Ann Graham Brock, begin about 7 minutes into the film. It raises awareness around what had happened to Mary Magdalene.

In this docu-film, Brock addresses the supposedly 7 demons that were cast out of Mary Magdalene. She points out that strangely, these demons are only mentioned in Luke and then copied in the longer, later ending of Mark. But Brock says that she read all the gospels she could, including the extra-canonical books that were found—and text after text, no one else mentions anything about it! We discussed earlier how we could tell that the Adam and Eve story was likely added to the Bible later because it also, uncharacteristically is not mentioned anywhere else. So, this text on Mary Magdalene may have been added later during an edit to discredit her in some way. More likely, in those days, even simple mental distress or physical illness could have been associated with demons. So, there's that too. Either way, a person doesn't jump from being raving mad and possessed, to "the woman who knows all" and "the woman in which wisdom is perfected more than all her brothers." It doesn't fit considering how evolved she was and interestingly, even Jesus was accused of having demons by the Pharisees in Matthew 12:24.

Cultural historian Kathleen Asbo shares another possible explanation, which I will share in the meditation section.

In the docu-film, we left it open as to whether or not Magdalene had been married to Jesus. I felt that it was possible, but there was no definitive proof. The ancient cultural traditions around burial rites had not been brought to my attention yet. Anne Barring states that, during that period, when it came to burial rituals, only the immediate family would have been allowed to perform those rites. This would be the duty of the wife, sister, or mother. So, for Mary Magdalene to have been involved in those rituals, she must have been his wife. Even the Gospel of John has Mary Magdalene at his tomb. In the Gospel of Luke, both Mary Madalene and Jesus' mother Mary were at the tomb, along with Joanna, who may have been Jesus' sister, according to Anne Baring.

John 20: 11-13

> But Mary stood at the sepulchre without,
> weeping. Now as she was weeping, she
> stooped down, and she looked into the
> sepulchre, And she saw two angels in white,
> sitting, one at the head, and one at the feet,
> where the body of Jesus had been laid. They
> say to her: Woman, why weepest though? She
> saith to them: Because they have taken away
> my Lord; and I know not where they have
> laid him.

There's also the Gospel of Philip that mentions that Jesus frequently kissed her. For this to be mentioned at all, it was likely more than the customary kiss when greeting someone. In our film, our main goal was to show what a wise female leader she was, so we didn't get into whether or not she was married to Jesus. The important point we wanted to make was that she was a powerful woman in her own right.

Recently, there was a feature film produced where Mary Magdalene was not portrayed as a prostitute or raving mad. She was shown as a deeply wise and intelligent woman. But Jesus was sorely miscast in this film with an actor who has excelled in other roles. His representation of Jesus was so poor it was distracting, and the film lost its impact. Still, it was an improvement on what we have had to watch before regarding Mary's incredible life.

The claim that there were no female apostles is what is used to still deny women the right to preach in many churches. If Jesus didn't see women fit, then that means they shouldn't be allowed to preach and spread his word. This is of course not true, from what I have read. Jesus had many women disciples, and he did call women to apostolic positions!

Besides the story of Mary, researchers have uncovered that there were other strong women leaders whose stories appear doctored, before and after the time of Jesus. There had been churches where these women held positions as founders, preachers, leaders, prophets, and apostles, and they have been kept out of our awareness. Once the church in Rome started to grow increasingly powerful and became the imperial church of Rome, rules were devised to take away the influence of these women, and steps were taken to diminish them or write them out of history entirely.

Ally Kateusz shared that the Council of Laodicea in 365 AD suddenly ruled that women weren't allowed so much as to enter the altar areas. These women were influential leaders and gifted prophetesses. What an outrage and shock that must have been for them. What were these mystics teaching us that needed to be suppressed? It had to have been something quite powerful for those desiring control to need to deprive them of it. By the 7th century, the Council of Nantes declared women "soulless beasts." It's these kinds of discoveries that now have contemporary men paying attention and exclaiming, "Oh, whoa. There was a problem and how did the shift of power and need to control women, our mothers and sisters, get so out of hand? How did that set us up for where we are today?"

By the 13th century, even Thomas Aquinas, who was otherwise quite wise, was brainwashed by those around him and was spreading this misogynistic view through his teachings. Aquinas was a follower of Aristotle, who wasn't Christian and was known to have issues with women, whom he called "defective and misbegotten," among other things.

With this, the domino effect was set into motion around how women were spoken of, perceived, and treated. But we need to remember that there was a time when the feminine was honored. There was a time when these brilliant women held leadership positions and contributed to humanity greatly. There was a time when we all had a Divine Mother. An imposed imbalance in power, along with a serious rewriting of history by the scribes had to take place to make them obscure to us now.

There Were Female Apostles

By now we are aware that the removal or degradation of the feminine didn't stop with the Holy Spirit. There is a pattern of removing or diminishing women in leadership positions.

We always hear about the 12 apostles, but there were actually more than that. Paul was an apostle for example, along with some others, including James and Junia. Junia was a highly regarded female apostle. Apostle Paul called her, "outstanding among the apostles". This presented a problem. The argument used to keep women from being allowed to lead or preach in church is that Jesus never chose any female apostles. What were they going to do about Apostle Junia? She was clearly named an apostle in Romans 16:7.

It seems the solution was that Junia would also undergo a sex change. The biblical redactors accomplished this with a quick sleight of hand, by adding an "s" to the end of her name. This gave it a masculine sounding ending. Thus, Apostle Junia became Apostle Junias. Problem solved. We would never have been the wiser! Luckily for us, older manuscripts were discovered with Junia's female name, revealing that this Apostle was a woman.

Another detail that gave away what was done is that the man's name Junias didn't even exist in ancient times! James Walters, in the Priscilla Papers, states: "Researchers have been unable to locate a single example of the male named Junias in ancient literature or inscriptions, either Latin or Greek."

Yet, there are still debates about whether or not Junia was an apostle to this day. Those who dispute her status reinterpret the translation of some words in that sentence changing her status. The counter argument is that, if the verse didn't say that Junia was an apostle, why did the scribes go through the trouble of masculinizing her name and adding the word "kinsmen"? In the 1899 Douay-Rheims Bible version that we have been using, the verse has the name changed to male:

"Salute Andronicus and Junias, my kinsmen
and fellow prisoners: who are of note among
the apostles, who were in Christ before me."

They are talking about two courageous apostles who were imprisoned for their beliefs—and one was a woman. Sure enough, we can see her name changed here.

Apostle Paul, who is often presented as an extreme misogynist, may also have been grossly misrepresented. It has always puzzled me when I would come across quotes of Paul speaking highly of the female apostles he worked with and then see quotes of horrible things he was to have said about women. It had me thoroughly confused—until I heard Elaine Pagels, the Harrington Spear Paine Professor at Princeton University, speak on the topic. In a talk about her book *The Gnostic Paul*, she mentioned that some of the writings/letters attributed to Paul were highly likely not written by him! Pagels says that the letters that were authenticated show that he valued and worked side-by-side respectfully with many women whom he held in high regard and spoke of splendidly as fellow apostles. Paul worked with many female apostles as equals, including Priscilla and Phoebe. The unvalidated letters have tarnished that image.

There was also Thecla, who traveled and taught with the Apostle Paul. Thecla passed tremendous trials and tribulations to fight for her right to teach and preach. Susan

E. Hylen calls her a modest apostle, and cultural historian, Kayleen Asbo shares a story in the *Who Framed Mary Magdalene?* docu-film, about a cave in Ephesus. On the cave wall, there is a painting of Paul and Thecla together; they both appear the same stature, showing equality, both with one of their hands in the air with their fingers in the exact same teaching mudra. Thecla's figure in the painting has been defaced, including the scraping off of her hand that was making the mudra symbol, in an apparent attempt to erase her authority and importance. Her apostle status is also disputed to this day, despite how revered she was. She is most frequently only given credit as Paul's eternal student, though her accomplishments speak for themselves.

We already know that Jesus commissioned Mary Magdalene directly, to go out and proclaim the news of his resurrection to the others. She was the first apostle! In the docu-film, Harvard scholar, Ann Graham Brock explains that what Jesus sent Mary to do puts her precisely in the role of an apostle. She gives the example that the word "apostle" means someone who is sent on someone else's behalf. Mary Magdalene became an apostle the moment Jesus sent her to go tell the others he had risen! Then, after telling the others, she continued to put Jesus' message further out into the world in her role as a commissioned apostle.

The Gospel of Mary and The Gospel of the Beloved Companion are where we find further evidence of her commission. However, even in three out of our traditional four canonical Gospels, it is written that Mary Magdalene was chosen as the first witness to the resurrection of Jesus and was asked by him to go and tell the others!

Brock mentions that some will agree that Mary is the Apostle to the Apostles but translate that to meaning something similar to having been a *secretary* to the male apostles. Her job was only to give them the message so they alone could do the actual apostle work. Instead of recognizing that she was afforded the highest honor of first witness and first commission. They explain away this colossal honor and have kept from giving her the status of true apostle who was appointed directly by Jesus himself! The reason for this denial is likely what we talked about before—if they admitted that Mary was the first apostle and other women were also chosen apostles, the male-run church can no longer keep women from preaching and becoming church leaders.

Many male and female theologians and scholars are stating that there is no reason women can't preach and hold leadership positions in church or the world, because Jesus himself demonstrated to us that women can and should.

Dramatic proof of this can be found in the Book of Acts. Craig D. Atwood writes of a scene in Acts that takes place at Pentecost, where the Holy Spirit descended upon the disciples giving them the ability to **preach** in other languages. Count Zinzendorf of Moravian Christianity asserts that this Book of Acts illuminated the fact that on that Day of Pentecost, over one hundred disciples, which included many women, were appointed to apostolic office. Atwood says other male theologians have missed that women were very much present in this group and that the New Testament itself specifies that there were female leaders in the early church. In his article, "Motherhood of the Holy Spirit in the 18th Century," he alerts us that Zinzendorf was one of the few preachers who understood that the Holy Spirit herself established "an equality in the teaching office between the sisters and brothers" in that very moment.

The Gospel of John

If you love the Gospel of John, you will likely enjoy the Gnostic Gospels. This is the Gospel among the canonical texts that many consider more gnostic in nature! This is because the rest of the canonical gospels give us a historical account of Jesus' life, whereas the Gospel of John gives us a spiritual account, which is in line with the Gnostic Gospels. It is very different in writing style as well. When I was young, the Gospel of John was my favorite canonical gospel, as it had a gentler more feminine, spiritual feel to it than the others. Sadly, it has gone through a noticeable amount of redaction. It is obvious that the writing style suddenly changes in spots. Even with the tinkering that happened, the Gospel of John is the most gnostic of the canonical Gospels. This Gospel always stood out for me, and many people recommend it to people who are new to Christianity as a first reading because of its loving gentleness.

There may be a good reason for it being so different from the other gospels. There is speculation it may have been copied from another gospel, with a few changes thrown in. Dr. Annine van der Meer has written about it, among others. She noted in her Ubiquity University talk that the Gospel of John has a striking resemblance to a Gospel most of us have never heard of, but I briefly mentioned earlier, The Gospel of the Beloved Companion. There are even parts that are identical to each other. The Gospel of the Beloved Companion is believed to be the older one of the two, written from a woman's perspective, by Mary Magdalene herself, hence the feminine tone. I share more about this Gospel next.

It is believed that the piecemeal feeling of the Gospel of John, compared to the natural flow of The Gospel of the

Beloved Companion is due to all of the edits required to downplay Mary Magdalene's prominence. How do we know that some of the parts that spoke of Mary Magdalene were changed in John? Recently, physical proof of some tinkering in that regard was discovered by Duke University doctoral student, Elizabeth Schrader. She was examining an image of Papyrus 66–commonly regarded as the oldest nearly fully intact manuscript of the Gospel of John. Schrader noticed a name, Mary or Maria, that had letters scratched out with new letters placed over them. These new letters now changed the name to read as Martha! In yet another verse a woman's name was changed to the word—sisters. She could physically see, upon extremely close examination, the changes right there on the papyrus paper!

After further inspection and many additional discoveries, she concluded that the name Mary was being changed to deliberately minimize the legacy of Mary Magdalene. The bigger placement Mary Magdalene had in this gospel was broken up and shared with two other women so that her role could be diluted and made to appear lesser. According to Schrader, Martha, from the Gospel of Luke, didn't even belong in the Gospel of John. The link to this article, "Mary or Martha?: A Duke Scholar's Research Finds Mary Magdalene Downplayed by New Testament Scribes" is included in the back of this book.

It is a mystery who the author or authors of the Gospel of John were. The reason many agree it could not have been John himself is that as a fisherman, it was almost certain that he was uneducated and illiterate. Many of the disciples weren't educated, which is not a problem at all. There have been talks about whether Jesus could read or write. Most conclude that, no, he likely could not read and even less likely that he could write, as it was mostly the upper class that learned those skills. Which may be another reason his teachings weren't written down by his followers. Most people were illiterate at that time. This just brings to our attention that it is not likely that John would have been the one to have written the Gospel. Many scholars agree that the Gospel of John was written by an anonymous person.

Mary Magdalene was thought to have been a woman of means, who was educated. It is therefore reasonable to believe that she wrote the Gospel of the Beloved Companion.

The Gospel of the Beloved Companion

The Gospel of the Beloved Companion: The Complete Gospel of Mary Magdalene is a recently published book containing what is said to be the first-century Gospel, also called, The Gospel According to the Beloved Companion, written from a woman's perspective, that of Mary Magdalene herself.

This is extremely exciting! It is a rare, first-person account, and it is written by a woman! It was written in Greek and brought from Egypt to the Languedoc, where it has been steadfastly preserved within the Essene Community of the translator, Jehanne de Quillan, since that period. Just to be clear, this is not the same as the Gospel of Mary, of which only fragments were found. This Gospel has been preserved, protected, and is nearly completely intact. Interestingly, according to Anne Baring's research, Jesus himself may have been brought up in an Essene community.

There is debate as to this Gospel's authenticity because the community that has kept it protected will not let it out of their hands. Would we, considering all that's happened to the other gospels? It seems they don't trust what could be done to it. I wonder if they are concerned it will be labeled inauthentic no matter what because of what it reveals. I'm just guessing here, as I do not have the answer. I do know that the Gospel of the Beloved Companion is wisely guarded and is the most poignant of all I have read. I mention this treasure here because it contains much of what may have been hidden from us or is missing from the Gospel of Mary fragments. We need to search within ourselves as to whether we believe it is authentic or not.

One of the main reasons I am convinced that this Gospel is authentic and came before many of the other gospels, is that partial verses from the very fluid Gospel of the Beloved Companion can be found in other gospels, especially in the Gospel of John.

According to Annine van der Meer's extensive research, writers and compositors of John may have obtained a copy of this earlier Gospel. It looks like they copied many parts, edited other parts, downgraded Mary Magdalene throughout, and then added a new Chapter 21 at the end. The Gospel of John seems to allude to John being the beloved companion. In the Gospel of the Beloved Companion, it is specific that Mary Magdalene was Jesus' beloved companion.

Another detail that convinces me that this Gospel is authentic and came first is that, as the original, the Gospel of the Beloved Companion has a much more beautiful, poetic, flow to it than the Gospel of John. It has the kind of flow that happens when there is only one author and no redactors involved in its writing! Many of our other gospels can feel piecemeal with various tones, which is what happens when there is editing by different scribes and different authors. That is not the case with this Gospel.

After translating the Gospel of the Beloved Companion, Jehanne de Quillan states that she is confident that it predates the canonical texts, which would have made it possible to copy.

The Gospel of the Beloved Companion brings something else to light. It talks of Jesus going to his wedding in Cana—not simply *a* wedding, as mentioned in the Gospel of John, but it says that he went to *his* wedding—Jesus' beloved companion was also his wife.

The Holy Spirit has a greater presence in this Gospel. Ruach (feminine spirit) is spoken of frequently. But Ruach was changed to Father in those parts that appear to have been copied to John.

This matches what Ally Kateusz disclosed to us in her book *Finding Holy Spirit Mother*, how scholar Sebastian P. Brock uncovered that Old Syriac scribes erased the word "Mother" in connection with the Holy Spirit out of the texts towards the end of the fourth century and inserted "Fathers" there instead. In the Gospel of John, the word Spirit was replaced. Now, even the best-meaning translators must work with that redacted text. This is one of the reasons why this unadulterated, genuine feeling Gospel of the Beloved Companion is so precious.

Jerry Kennell shares the heart of the beautiful Gospel in his article "What is Truth?"

> He writes:
> "The clear and consistent message of Jesus's teaching in this gospel is simple, yet deep and very beautiful. It is this: The Kingdom of Heaven is within you, a seed of the Living Spirit waiting to be discovered, nurtured and cultivated. And it is to be lived into the world outside you."

Originally hesitant to read this Gospel, I found myself immersed and overwhelmed with emotions upon its exploration. The wisdom it contains can initiate an opening to Spirit again, to the fullness of God, and the wonder of our existence.

The Gnostic Gospels

It took me a while to accept that there were differing views as to what Jesus' teachings were. At first, I didn't like hearing that, because I love definitive answers. "You mean the Gospels in the Bible were chosen by leaders of that time, and there had been other ways of understanding Jesus' teachings?" Yes, there were many. For some readers, this new information being presented may have the same effect it originally had on me. In that case, you may need to give yourself time, as I did, to digest it. I was not happy at first. There were other ways of looking at Jesus' shared wisdom! No one had all the answers—hence all the debates and discussions! I longed for a well-defined belief system. At that time, I didn't want to explore. What if I get it wrong? With something this big, I wanted all the clear answers from the get-go.

Any teaching that is different from what is found in the canonical Bible or church dogma is considered heretical. The word "heresy" used to make me nervous. Heresy is always presented in such a way that implies that its meaning is that something is bad or false. But if we look it up, it means that we are talking about something that doesn't line up with or conflicts with the popular, accepted opinion or doctrine; it varies from orthodox belief.

Perhaps a desire for controlled organization and clarity is what brought about the creation of the New Testament. Only a handful of gospels were chosen. I now realize it would have been incredibly beneficial to have more insights into Jesus' life and teachings to get an even deeper sense of what Jesus' messages were. It is devastating how much we lost forever regarding what he shared, his teachings, and his life. Thousands of years later, all we can do is gather as much information as possible and do our best with what we have. Our Bible remains incredibly sacred to us for the wisdom it contains. Wouldn't we love to know what the edits were that befell it? Could the rejected gospels possibly provide some hints? There must have been some overlap.

The good news is that we now do have at least some more insights into Jesus' teachings available to us through the discovery of a few hidden gospels that were unearthed in a tiny village called Nag Hammadi. We are lucky they were hidden before they could be destroyed! What a blessing! These gospels had originally been part of all the gospels that existed before they were separated and labeled canonical or Gnostic. Remember, everything outside of the canonical ended up being put into a bin labeled Gnostic, whether they were similar or not. Not every one of them fits all the criteria for being Gnostic.

For example, the Gnostics were known to believe in two different Gods, a supreme, benevolent God and a malevolent lesser God, who created the material world and who is usually associated with the God in the Old Testament. This belief in two different Gods is not part of any of the gospels labeled Gnostic that I researched.

When I look up Gnostic Gospels on the internet, I have come across some Christian websites where the most extreme diversions from canonical understanding are cited, which don't reflect the brunt of the Gnostic Gospels. This is likely done to put them all in a bad light. Most of the so-called Gnostic Gospels I have read are beautiful and focus on Jesus' love-based teachings. They are both gentle and empowering, with a spiritual focus. There are a few rare exceptions that are bizarre, but they have not much to do with the others. Keep in mind the vastly differing opinions among Christians that were taking place, this is also evident among the groups called Gnostic—there are different philosophies there as well.

The Gospel of Mary and the Gospel of Thomas are among those worth reading for a more expansive impression of what Jesus taught and a more detailed picture of his life. When translated correctly, Jesus talks about the Holy Spirit as his "true Mother." Though the Gospel of Mary follows a similar structure as the Gnostic dialogues, neither of these Gospels shares the classic dualism, the creation account, and a couple of other elements usually associated with the Gnostics. In these Gospels there is one benevolent God, the same as in the canonical texts.

One difference I did notice is that Gnostics don't see sin in the same way as more orthodox Christians. According to many Gnostic groups, sin comes from ignorance. The two go hand in hand. So, obtaining gnosis, or wisdom, would keep humanity from sinning and suffering. Though ultimately God is incomprehensible, gnosis would also bring us into a closer relationship with God. According to them, Jesus brings us gnosis.

Another significant difference between the canonical texts and the more Gnostic type of texts are that the Gnostic texts are spiritual rather than historical in nature, as was mentioned before, and there is a difference in the focus of salvation. In the canonical Gospels, we understand that Jesus having died on the cross for us is what brings us salvation. Since Jesus died for our sins, simply believing in Jesus saves us, no matter what we've done, though we are encouraged to live by his word.

Sadly, there were also some redactions in the Gnostic texts that took place. Finding the untarnished spiritual guidance and finding our Mother can be a challenge even in some of them. In her book *Finding Holy Spirit Mother,* Ally Kateusz shares that Sebastian P. Brock from the University of Oxford, who authored many books on Early Syrian Christianity, exposed how towards the end of the fourth century Old Syriac scribes began erasing out of the texts the word Mother in connection with the Holy Spirit and started inserting Fathers instead. We can't pretend that this was accidental, and we can never uncover all the alterations.

For instance, it was discovered that scribes removed not only the feminine pronouns, but sentences containing nouns describing the Holy Spirit. Scribes removed a sentence from the Acts of Phillip. Kateusz says that in this instance, scribes completely deleted a verse of Mary Magdalene's. In the older versions of the Acts of Phillip, we would have read that Mary Magdalene spoke about us being guilty of forgetting our origins, our Father in Heaven, and our spiritual Mother. But if we were to wake up, we would receive illumination. The scribes took out the part about the Mother and replaced it with something that spoke of the Father only. Brock says there is distinct evidence that this was done to many gospels! The scribes added and removed entire sentences or words and added pronouns—you get the picture. By the 7th century, any sign of our beautiful Mother Holy Spirit had disappeared.

When people argue against the Holy Spirit being female, these heavily redacted gospels are used to prove their point! Which makes it hard to argue. Even here, in some of the Gnostic Gospels the Holy Spirit/Shekinah who was always associated with Wisdom and who was described as the Invisible Soul of the Cosmos has been erased. Look around and see the colossal impact it has had on our world. But if we are diligent and look hard, in the older, unedited versions of preserved gospels and writings, we can still find her, our Mother, the Holy Spirit.

There was even a time when Pope Innocent III forbade anyone from owning or reading the Bible unless they were clergy. If they did, it was under the penalty of death. There has been much spiritual wisdom kept from the people.

Some of the Gnostic Gospels still speak of the Holy Spirit and the Divine Feminine has a presence. They reveal the position of leadership given to Mary Magdalene, who received the secret teachings from Jesus due to her greater capacity to understand. All this information the gospels contained is likely why, at least partially, they weren't included in the canonical Gospels.

Then, there is the Gospel of Thomas. Let's take a look at an unusual gospel, which is probably even older and written closer to Jesus' time than the canonical Gospels. It is not seen as a true Gnostic Gospel. The content is very much canonical in nature, but it was left out of the Bible. Rather than a narrative, it is a book of Jesus' sayings and parables. Most now believe that the reason this Gospel got mislabeled as Gnostic is the simple fact that it was found concealed with the bundle of Gnostic Gospels that were discovered in Nag Hammadi.

There's one saying that gets talked about often. Saying 101 from the Gospel of Thomas has Jesus likely talking about his physical mother, Mary, and his spiritual mother, the Holy Spirit. I say likely because a of couple the words on the papyrus seem to be illegible or missing. The saying starts with what one mother did for or gave Jesus. What that was specifically is the part we need to guess at. Different translators fill in the blanks differently. We usually see words referring to having "born or birthed his body" placed there. Then the saying goes on to say that Jesus' True Mother gave him life! He is speaking of his Mother the Holy Spirit there.

The Gospel of Phillip also declares that whoever becomes a Christian "gains both a father and a mother."

We can also find our Mother Holy Spirit's powerful presence in the Acts of Thomas, where she is called "the Mother of all creation!"

Many of the gospels found at Nag Hammadi are worthy of reading for a more expansive, heart-opening understanding of Jesus' teachings. Elaine Pagels wrote a book called, *The Gnostic Gospels* that gives us a condensed overview of them. We will discover that many Gnostic scholars believe that Jesus never set out to create an organized religion. Rather, Jesus incarnated to teach us how to live and how to evolve spiritually ourselves. We are encouraged to learn from God and Jesus through direct revelation—meaning mysticism and a more direct relationship with God. These teachings and experiences are believed to take us on a path to inner spiritual knowledge and transformation that will end ignorance, and when ignorance ends, so does suffering.

Jesus himself shared a deeper gnosis, in the form of secret teachings that he bestowed upon his closest, wisest disciples. He was careful to give those powerful teachings only to those spiritually mature enough to understand.

To the public, Jesus spoke mostly in parables and metaphors to keep his message simpler, not revealing the depths and mysteries that most of humanity wasn't ready for yet. How Jesus taught the public, compared to his select group of disciples, differed for good reasons. If the uninitiated or people who are not advanced enough spiritually got ahold of these teachings, they could be led astray by misunderstanding them. Also, people who dive too far into the mystical before being ready can literally lose their minds. Jesus wisely taught at the level of people's capacity to comprehend. By doing this, he taught in digestible pieces, while also planting seeds that could grow to a higher understanding later. At this critical time in history, humanity is being called to slowly start opening ourselves up to the spiritual and mystical again. What can these gospels teach us?

What the Inclusive Bible Reveals

All of the gospels become more meaningful when more accurately translated from Aramaic or Greek, the way they have done in The Inclusive Bible. It doesn't mean that we are not still working with redacted material, we are, but this Bible does address the Spirit as she was addressed in the original language of the Bible—as a feminine being. They additionally found less sexist ways to convey the same ancient truths. We still can't know where all of the Mothers were taken out, but this Bible version feels more accurate than the others we have—and it reveals something to us that was once obscured!

There's a passage in the Gospel of John, that Deidre Havrelock posted on her website of the same name, using The Inclusive Bible to show how beautiful it is when accurate language is used for the Holy Spirit. Upon reading that text, I discovered something else—this Bible version makes it clear that Jesus is speaking in John of what happened to Wisdom, aka the Holy Spirit and Spirit of Truth, after her temple was destroyed! I encourage you to go to the front of this book where we quote Sirach (Ecclesiasticus)—to see how, when we change the "he's" to "she's" in the John 14: 15-18 Bible verses, the way they accurately did in The Inclusive Bible, we recognize that we are talking about the rejection and loss of identity of the same person in Sirach! We would never know to make the connection to the Old Testament's Wisdom when reading the New Testament, where they changed the Spirit of Truth's gender! In the Douay-Rhimes-1899 Bible Version below, if we hadn't manually made the corrections, showing everyone the "she's" that would have originally been present instead of the "he's, we would never know who Jesus was talking about or what event he is referring to. With the proper, original gender in place, that's when we see that Jesus is talking about what happened to Wisdom when the world stopped recognizing her! See below.

John 14: 15-18

> If you love me, keep my commandments. And I will ask the Father, and he shall give you another Paraclete, that he [**she**] may abide with you for ever. The spirit of truth, whom the world cannot receive, because it seeth him [**her**] not, nor knoweth him [**her**] but you shall know him [**her**]; because he [**she**] shall abide with you, and shall be in you. I will not leave you orphans, I will come to you.

Christian Mystics and Prophets

Prophets often receive a direct call to service from the Divine for the sake of humanity. The visions and wisdom of the mystics and prophets of the Bible are of such great value to us because their insights come from direct revelation—through direct communication with the Divine. In our current culture where many of our goals are to get to the top, the incredible honor of being of service can sound like a burden. We associate servitude with something lowly, which couldn't be more opposite from the truth. Jesus himself has been called a servant leader. He encourages us to be of service too. That is the path to a meaningful and impactful life.

Our greatest spiritual leaders are unfortunately often shunned in society. The Bible shares that prophets are not recognized in their "hometown". This creates an obstacle to getting their message out or to performing miracles there, to be sure. The familiarity of the prophet breeds contempt and disbelief. Even Jesus had this issue. People who knew him well while growing up, said, "Messiah? What? Isn't that just Mary and Joseph's son?"

Luke 4:24

> And he said: Amen I say to you, that no
> prophet is accepted in his own country.

Mark 6:4

> And Jesus said to them: A prophet is not
> without honor, but in his own country, and in
> his own house and among his own kindred.

There was a great propensity to diminish the insights of female mystics and prophets by casting doubt on them or erasing them from our stories. Many were persecuted for their gifts. Both Jesus and Mary Magdalene were prophets and mystics of the highest caliber. Today, mystics and people who can see beyond the veil are often not taken seriously.

The cosmos has multiple dimensions. All dimensions are part of the whole, as nothing is outside of Spirit. We have sadly become so focused on only the physical, material and the mental part of life, that often we have on blinders to the rest of existence. We are missing out on something precious beyond words. There is so much more, and we need to become aware of what lies beyond again, to help us heal.

The biggest misconception about other planes of existence is that they are somewhere "out there" apart from us. In her book *Eye of the Heart*, Rev. Dr. Cynthia Bourgeault talks of her visits to the imaginal realm she takes by journeying inward—this wondrous place lies within us! Imaginal does not mean imaginary. The imaginal realm is real. It is inopportune that the two words sound so similar. She defines the imaginal realm as a place bordering between the visible and invisible worlds—perceivable through the eye of our hearts. We need to become more heart-focused.

Prophets and mystics can receive Divine information from the beings in these worlds in the form of puzzle pieces or through symbolism—which means they still need to filter these messages through their lenses of perception. Each will have varying levels of understanding of what is revealed to them. Our Divine Mother may not have been or be perceivable by all. One would likely need to be open to her, and it would need to be the right time.

Jesus shares about forces and beings of good and evil in the Bible. He confronts demons more than once. These forces are recognized in shamanism and other mystical traditions as well. Practicing mysticism, therefore, is not to be entered into lightly. It is a significant undertaking.

Margaret Barker reveals in her book, *The Great High Priest*, that there was much more to Jesus' teachings than recorded in the canonical Gospels. She confirms that it was understood for centuries that Jesus shared a secret tradition that he taught to only those few of his followers who were ready! He knew better than to share it with people who weren't far enough along in their spiritual evolution, as it could do harm under those circumstances. Mary Magdalene was the disciple who was said to understand these advanced teachings the most completely, which caused much jealousy from some of the other disciples—especially Peter.

Barker also mentions a quotation from Epiphanius, from the fourth century, where it declares that the Gospel of Egyptians was a book with "odd sayings" that came secretly from Jesus. One such saying was that all three—the Father, Holy Spirit, and Jesus—are the same person. Which, at first seems strange. Jesus incarnated as the Son and spoke of both his Father and his Mother, yet they are all three the same person—the one, same God. Yet the individual expressions are still vitally important.

The great prophet Jeremiah's book in the Old Testament is said to have gone through so much editing that it is close to impossible to know when you are reading Jeremiah's words or the words of the editors. That is why theologians and scholars like Margaret Barker are so important. She realizes that each group behind each book has its own agenda, highlighting certain information, and omitting other significant parts. She, with her vast biblical knowledge, cross references and fills in some of what was left out. We still won't entirely know what was taken out in places.

Some pieces can be put back together this way though, so we get a better sense of what was originally being conveyed by making educated guesses. What I find moving is that mystics from other religions so often said similar things to what the Christian mystics and prophets said, they just used different names, languages, and traditions. There are common threads among most all religions.

I love exploring the female prophets, such as Sarah, the first Matriarch, and the Mother of Nations, who is presented in the Jewish Midrash as a powerful prophet. Then there are the prophets Deborah, Hannah, Miriam, Huldah, Abigail, and Ester. I wish there was more written about them so we could get to know them better.

When we talk about Abraham and Sarah, most people know that Abraham was a great prophet, but not everyone realizes that Sarah was revered as a priestess and prophet. I do wonder how much editing befell her story. There is no way to know. What we do know is that Sarah is the only woman in the Bible whose name God changed! She went from Sarai, meaning "princess," to Sarah, "mother of nations." We know that Sarah's great beauty, even later at an older age, had Abraham fearing the pharaoh may kill him just for a chance to possess her. He asked Sarah not to say that they were married. The pharaoh did take her as his, as anticipated, but then God intervened and Abraham got his wife back.

We read that Sarah was at first unable to have children, so she gave her handmaiden Hagar to her husband to birth his child. This was not uncommon in those days. Then, well after the age one expects for it to be possible to become pregnant, according to God's promise, Sarah herself gave birth to a son named Isaac—with whom God made an everlasting covenant. Now Abraham had two sons.

Savina J. Teubal, author of the book *Sarah the Priestess: The First Matriarch of Genesis,* says that the story of Sarah can become confusing because it is told from a patriarchal point of view, though the times weren't fully patriarchal yet! She deems that during the time of Sarah, society was transitioning from a matriarchal society to a patriarchal one—bridging pre-history and the recorded history we start with in the Bible. Often people don't realize that civilization started long before the recording of the Bible. From the Paleolithic era, around 20,000 BC, through to around 500 BC, the Great Mother, the Great Goddess, was worshipped and recognized as the one who birthed our world and the entire cosmos. After that, things started changing by force. She explains that the women in Sarah's time were struggling to maintain their traditions and customs, which were at odds with their husbands' or fathers' push for new patriarchal ways. Teubal also feels that much of Sarah's life, along with the writings on the power and wisdom she had were likely removed from the pages, which contributes to the unclarity of the story.

When we get to the part that we all have come to know—regarding the relationship of Sarah and Hagar, Teubal concludes that the text was distorted via redactions and faulty patriarchal interpretations, which often made women appear conniving instead of powerful.

According to scholarly literature, Sarah had treated Hagar quite well. Whenever women came to visit Sarah, for example, she made sure they paid a visit to Hagar too, and so on. But after some time, when Hagar was pregnant with Abraham's child, she started acting condescendingly towards Sarah. So, an issue arose. The tale is then often presented as if Sarah mercilessly sent Hagar and her son out into the desert in a fit of anger, which doesn't make sense considering Sarah's standing, wisdom, and good character. Teubal states that Sarah was likely a highest-ranking priestess who was simply following the codes and laws of the period. First, Sarah was securing her son's inheritance. Then, Hagar, who had previously gone from handmaiden status to slave status, was now being given her freedom. Teubal explains, "Sarah's action, with the God's approval results not from an emotional state but from adherence to a form of legalistic tradition," which is why Abraham was told to do as Sarah says.

Genesis 21:12

> And God said to him: Let it not seem
> grievous to thee for the boy, and for thy
> bondswoman: in all that Sara hath said to
> thee, hearken to her voice...

Other female scholars have also shared that they believe a negative spin was put on the story because what is written doesn't reflect women's cooperative relationships in those times, even if, in this case, a possible conflict arose. And let's remember, God had promised that Hagar and Ishmael would be unharmed and that Ishmael would raise a great nation of his own. Sarah had the wisdom that the two of them were going to be safe!

There were other mystics and prophets later throughout the ages as well and we know a little more about some of them. Hildegard of Bingen comes to mind. She was a brilliant, German, Benedictine abbess and highly respected mystic, during the high Middle Ages. Hildegard of Bingen was also a polymath. She was a writer, composer, philosopher, and a gifted intuitive medical writer and practitioner.

She was said to have counseled bishops, popes, and kings when they came to her for sagacious wisdom and guidance. This Christian mystic nun spoke often of her encounters with Mother God. Hildegard was heavily influenced by Augustine, however, which did affect her frame of reference she viewed her visions through. Still, she made immense contributions to society, especially around natural medicines and the environment. Later, for centuries she was ridiculed, in an attempt to discredit her, but she has gained back her well-deserved respect. Her plant medicine knowledge is still used to this day.

Here was this brilliant, mystic nun, yet we have been taught to shun mysticism as Christians. We have heard the stories of the 3 kings who followed the star to Jesus' manger. But in fact, the words used here to describe these men, translate better to "wise men from the East" who were known as astrologers. Yet we have been taught that astrology is evil, rather than something that can lend us guidance, much like a useful weather report when done properly by skilled professionals. We have been taught to disregard things that can help us.

Mysticism certainly is not to be taken lightly or jumped into like a fad, which is how some people have approached it. The mystical journey, if embarked upon, is to be treated with great respect, reverence, caution, and patience. Simply meditating can, with time, already open us to a broader cosmic perspective.

It is said that when Einstein was an old man, he was asked before his death if he had any regrets? He was to have answered, "I wish I had read more of the mystics earlier in life." That is not something one expects to hear from a scientist. It sounds like he discovered that he received information through their insights and visions that coincided with his scientific discoveries, taking the understanding of those breakthroughs further than possible by using science alone.

Mysticism is a journey and there is much to learn and digest, so we need to take our time. It requires patience and occasionally misinterpretations can happen, even by experienced mystics. If one is inexperienced, these misinterpretations are even more likely. I remember reading about a young man who had a one-time brief encounter with a compassionate male spirit, and he assumed he had encountered the Holy Spirit, making the argument now that the Holy Spirit was male. With mystical experiences, many of the spirit guides first encountered are often male. When contacted by the Holy Spirit, however, there will be no doubt whose presence one is in, with her lyrical, female voice, more beautiful than words can ever describe.

Upon reflecting, I sense that when the Holy Spirit's temple was destroyed and she was exiled from our consciousness, even some of the mystics were no longer able to recognize her true essence and her femininity, until the time for her return—and that time has come!

All of society would benefit if we slowed down our lives, turned off technological devices more often, and respectfully and heartfully, tuned in to the rhythms and mysteries of the universe around us for a sense of direction, in both personal and global matters. The divine connection to God is needed to navigate the challenges of climate change and other complex issues before us. Using only our physical resources to save this planet will never be enough. We unequivocally need to recognize that we are part of God and respectfully, without rushing haphazardly in, tune into the spiritual and mystical for necessary Divine help and guidance.

Part 2: The Present Day

Effects of Removing Our Divine Mother on Humanity and Planetary Health

We are living at the most pivotal time in history. Never has humanity been in this position before. We are at a tipping point. We, the people living on this planet at this very moment, are being called upon. We are the last ones who have the chance to turn things around. We have the honor of being the ones entrusted with the commission of helping to heal the planet. So, in some ways, these are exciting times.

We need to take immediate action, which means getting over the illusion that simply posting our opinions on social media is the same as acting. Social media has been putting us to sleep. Time to wake up. There is much to do, and it is going to require massive numbers of people from all walks of life stepping up to the plate to work together.

No time for sticking our heads in the sand. Animals are going extinct 1,000 times faster than ever in history due to the way we are treating them and all of nature. This is a forewarning of what will befall us. Humans may be the first species to bring about their own extinction. Can we turn things around? Only if we try.

The truth is that there have been extinctions before. The nature of nature is that it is ever-changing. But this accelerated destruction is our doing. Our failure to recognize that all of life is sacred is at the heart of the destruction.

To initiate substantial healing, we must return our Divine Mother to her rightful place next to our Father, by bringing the wise, peacemaking, empathetic feminine principles back into the world's consciousness. To really understand what that means, we need to understand that we have regressed as a society in a few areas. We most certainly have made progress scientifically on many levels. We can get a person on the moon. From that vantage point, we can see that our planet isn't physically flat. We are capable of computers, creating artificial intelligence, etc.

But we have regressed as a humanity when it comes to realizing the "non-flatness" of the cosmos and its spiritual layers. If we take a moment to grasp just how intricate, and complex the world is and how everything fits together in just the right way to make it all possible and work, the idea that it all fell into place by chance feels absurd. But do we give enough thought to what that means? What are the multiple layers to existence? And why aren't we paying nearly enough attention to what is beyond the physical?

Recently I came across a documentary, *Is Genesis History?* This film scientifically explains why the evolution theory—and that is all it is, a theory—has huge holes in it, and doesn't add up entirely. Some parts add up, but not everything. After watching the film, I had more questions than answers, but I was open. I was open to Spirit; I was open to the miracle of God's work. I was open to the possibility of multiple dimensions and depths of existence that we have lost touch with in our fast-paced, noisy, modern world. Our perspective has narrowed so much that, in that state, we can't possibly find the answers and solutions that we are looking for. We need to build a more daily, intimate, loving relationship with God. We need to honor and tune in to the spiritual.

We also want to look at the type of knowledge that is currently running the world, because the priorities that come with it have been running it into the ground! The current atmosphere of greed, corruption, our feeling separate from God, each other, and the cosmos will keep us from doing what needs to be done to heal. When we call upon the Holy Spirit, we will once again be able to tune into the higher knowledge that comes from her wisdom. We will be able to see our lives and the world in a fresh, more conscious light.

With corporate corruption and so much concentrated power at the top, we are in an out-of-balance patriarchal state, run by out-of-balance patriarchal qualities. Naming these qualities or energies and how they were traditionally viewed will help us get started on the path of healing.

Man and woman, the feminine and masculine energies brought about at the very beginning of creation, were not designed to be polarizing. That wasn't the plan at all. They were always meant to be complementary, mutually supporting, and balancing. For that, they need to be equal. One can't be controlling the other. One isn't more important than the other. They are reciprocal to each other. The world goes off kilter when they are not in balance, because then the lower qualities of the prevailing quality become unchecked, and that is what has happened in our world. The knowledge of these energies and principles comes from ancient wisdom. Most religions and spiritualities speak of them, emphasizing how the *integration* of these qualities brings equilibrium and wholeness.

We see this in the classic yin and yang symbol, where the black feminine side includes a portion of the white in its middle, meaning the feminine contains some of the masculine. When we look at the white masculine side, we see that it contains a circle of black, representing that it is important and healthy for the masculine to contain some of the feminine. The yin and yang symbol is showing us that nothing in existence is ever all male or all female.

Notice also that the yin and the yang are not separated by a hard, straight line, which would be divisive or polarizing feeling. No. The two sides are intentionally separated by a soft 's-curve', creating a gentle dance, and flow between the two sides. They are supportive of each other, harmonizing, and beautifully fluid.

We already discussed how the feminine was demoted, likely with the intent of diminishing women's power, not grasping that we and the entire world are an intricate meshwork of both qualities—when one of them is diminished, everyone and everything that exists is negatively impacted. Einstein said everything is energy. That's true because everything is God. We can now imagine how when half of that energy is suppressed it throws all of existence off balance, not only women—though, girls and women get the worst of it.

Let's look at the masculine and feminine qualities to see what needs restoring to bring about the kind of global healing that will help save our planet. By identifying which qualities are considered feminine, we can uncover what has been suppressed and devalued for thousands of years. Much of society had come to accept the unfairness and imbalance and the damage has been immense. We are changing that now.

Just as certain physical traits are feminine or masculine, there are also soul qualities seen as masculine or feminine. A few *physical* examples of masculinity would be that men tend to be hairier and can grow beards. Men also have considerably stronger, denser muscles than women, as well as denser bones.

Examples of some *physical* feminine qualities would be that women have an inner reproductive system with a uterus. They can conceive life and give birth. Our muscles are less strong, and they and our bones are smaller in size and in density than men's, except for our hips, which may be wider, due to our pelvises needing to allow for the birth of babies.

There is a correlation between our physical structure and our spiritual qualities. A woman's physical body is designed to receive the man. Her sexual organs are inside of her, so when having sex, she allows the man inside of her. That makes for a very intimate sexual act for the woman. When describing feminine spiritual qualities, one of them is receptivity. Men's genitals are on the outside of the body, putting men in the giving position. It then becomes a blissful mutual exchange, when done consciously.

Though we are equal, we are clearly not the same. We are different in the most exciting ways, and it all has a purpose. We maintain balance on this planet, and were meant to love, complement, protect, and help each other. That does not mean that we need to complement each other in a rigidly outlined manner. In a relationship, how we complement and help each other is as individual as there are people on earth.

We bring much impetus to each other's lives intellectually, emotionally, physically, and spiritually. Our brains are beautiful, unique, patchwork quilts made of male and female qualities. Men tend to have more of the male qualities and women more of the female qualities, but occasionally, it is the other way around. There is room for great variations. No two people are alike, and the brain is malleable as we transform and grow. If we are seeking someone who is a good life partner for us, with patience we will likely find them. We were meant to help and support each other to evolve and transform, as well as bring joy to each other's lives.

Each of the feminine and masculine archetypes conveys important positive traits we need individually, and as a humanity. Each archetype contains lower expressions as well. Any of these qualities can become negative and destructive if not kept in check and in balance through the opposite archetype's qualities.

The feminine archetype is characterized by being, bringing such qualities as harmony, compassion, empathy, grace, thoughtfulness, nurturing, peacekeeping, flow, restoration, intuition, creativity, inner connection, and so on. The masculine archetype is characterized by doing and is said to bring ambition, action, logic, assertiveness, courage, competition, strength, focus, discipline, confidence, protectiveness, structure, and so on. A wounding has happened between these two energies that asks to be healed. It is no small matter because they are the core of all existence.

To heal humanity, we need to bring our loving Mother Holy Spirit back into our consciousness so she may pour her Divine qualities into the world in balance with the

Divine Masculine. In unison, they can heal. This will help us see the way to making wiser choices that benefit all of humanity. With the many changes made to our texts and with the misinterpretations of our scriptures, we can bet we have been getting some critical things wrong. We need all the resources available to us, so we may stop and seriously reevaluate what we are doing. If we address the spiritual and physical issues that lay before us, it would then become possible to heal and transform our world.

Effects of Removing Our Divine Mother on Girls and Women

We have our work cut out for us. We first need to face what has gone wrong, before we can heal.

Fathers of girls, sons who love their mothers, brothers who care about their sisters, and husbands who love their wives—please listen with all your hearts. As long as our Mother, the feminine part of God remains missing, making it so anyone feminine is not fully recognized as part of the Divine, girls and women won't be safe in this world! Consciously or unconsciously, the omission, along with the Adam and Eve story, has wrongly diminished the value of the lives of girls and women for thousands of years. This is being used as an excuse to perpetrate violence against them across the world. Even here in the U.S., domestic violence against women, human trafficking, rape, and murder are all part of the consequences of the devaluing of the feminine.

The high rate of infanticide of baby girls and gender-specific abortions in places such as India and China are still so prevalent that in some of those countries now, there aren't enough young women for the young men to marry!

Even in America girls and women haven't been afforded the same opportunities in life, which means they often aren't able to live as complete a life. With a reduced number of opportunities, they are not able to contribute their gifts to society to their full capacity.

If we have someone we love, wouldn't we wish for them to be safe, valued, heard, and have the type of opportunities that bring a full, happy, and purposeful life? The Bible was edited to exert control. It's critical to bring back the feminine's original reflection in God, and with that, bring back our mutual value.

Returning our Mother Holy Spirit to reside with our Father will positively affect both how girls and women see themselves, and how the world sees them. Honoring women as equals does not mean that they are the same as men. The feminine and the masculine each bring complementary gifts of great value to the table. We can appreciate the differences between the male and female, the yin and yang, while also celebrating their equal value—deserving equal respect and equal opportunity for equal quality of life.

When I was in high school, our psychology teacher asked our class to choose a side of the room to stand on— on one side were the students who felt women's liberation was important for women and on the other side were the students who felt a woman's place was in the home. I stood on the home side, because that is what I had been raised with and because I could hardly wait to be a wife, mother, and homemaker. That was what I truly loved. I loved to cook, bake, garden, embroider, oil paint, and create a cozy home and care for my family. I didn't realize what they were fighting for until later down the line when I tried to share my God-given, creative gift of storytelling with the world through filmmaking. As a capable filmmaker and believer in the impact story can have on humanity, I was ready to contribute, with wisdom and passion in my heart. Only, I discovered that women were basically shut out of this creative and influential profession. Therefore, I have since changed my position from my high school self. Though I still love all those things I loved before, I long to share something of additional value with humanity that I am not being given the opportunity to do. It is soul-crushing to have those walls constructed for us, to be put in boxes that tell us where we are allowed to stay, while the world is wide open for our male counterparts. It is soul-crushing that we have great gifts we came in with, that go unshared.

There are those stories of women who accomplished big things against all odds. But that should be the norm, not the rare exception! There are those hero women who have created incremental breakthroughs for women in big and small ways. There were common pleasures we weren't allowed to participate in. I remember the story of Bobbi Gibb, who at 23 was the first woman to run the Boston Marathon in 1966. Her race application was declined. The reason given by the race director was that women were not physiologically capable of running marathon distances. The rules for amateur sports drawn up by the AAU clearly stated women were not permitted to run more than a mile and a half competitively. In hindsight, we realize how ridiculous this rule of exclusion was. Trust me, there are many more like this, spoken and unspoken, that still exist for women.

Being told she couldn't run made her all the more determined to do so! Sporting her brother's Bermuda shorts, a swimsuit top, and a hooded sweatshirt—with the hood up— she waited for the race to start. She jumped into the group when about half the men had passed, from a covering on the sidelines. Worried about what would happen once some of the guys running noticed there was a woman racing with them, she was pleasantly surprised to find that they were friendly and encouraging. As time went on, she commented to one of the men that she was overheating due to the hoodie, but was afraid to take it off because if it was discovered that she was a woman, she would be extracted from the race. The man took a stand and said that he wouldn't let that happen!

Soon others backed her as well. Feeling safe, she removed the hooded sweatshirt. To her delight, when the crowd realized a woman was running, they all started cheering! Humanity is basically great! So who are the people exacting the control and doing the harm?

After the race, Governor John Volpe proudly shook her hand—while later the race director, tried adamantly to cast doubt that she had even run the race at all! Two very different responses to the same situation. Soon after, the title of a *Record American* article read "Roberta Gets Official Support: Females May Run Marathon". It was decided that women could run. I love this story, as it reminds us of how women have been gaining simple rights so we can walk out from the sidelines and more fully into life!

Unfortunately, there are far more situations with more painful outcomes. Throughout history, often when women had great accomplishments or were prime contributors to successful endeavors, men got the credit! My mind goes to Jocelyn Bell Burnell, whose supervisor won the Nobel Peace Prize for her discovery of pulsars. I think of Microbiologist Esther Lederberg, with her Stanford University Master's in genetics, who discovered the Lambda Phage virus, which gave us a new understanding of viruses that we still work with currently. She later partnered with her husband and their joint work led to the discovery that bacteria can exchange DNA and form a new strain. Her husband alone got the credit for their discovery, and he alone received the Nobel Peace Prize for the work they performed side-by-side. There is something painfully wrong with this picture.

Speaking of women and medicine. Studies show that women still have a harder time being heard or taken seriously at the doctor's office. This can lead to dire consequences.

To make matters worse, originally most medical research was done on men. Since women's anatomy is different, our symptoms can be different, doctors didn't take many women's health concerns seriously, including warning signs of a heart attack, because they didn't fit in with what they'd learned to look for in men. Women who were justifiably concerned with a health issue were often dismissed as being guilty of hypochondria or hysteria. Dangerous indicators were disregarded until it was too late. Women of color have an even harder having their conditions taken seriously and treated.

This is slowly improving as we try to raise awareness, but it is not yet resolved, because it's attitudinal. It isn't just about a woman trying to be taken seriously for her own health either. A mother's intuition or keen observation skills can be rejected, instead of honored. A mother has a way of knowing when something is wrong with their child. I remember reading a heartbreaking story, where a young mother in her early 20s brought her extremely sick toddler to the emergency room explaining she was concerned that something was life-threateningly wrong with her son. She was told that she was overreacting and sent home. This courageous and loving young mother went back again, as the feeling in her heart grew more desperate, and pled with the hospital staff to please take another look, there was something terribly wrong with her child. Criticized for being a hysterical, inexperienced mom, the doctors sent them home again. She frantically came back a third time, where her young son died of meningitis in the waiting room. Not being heard or respected in the same way men are, can have detrimental consequences.

Uneven relationships are not healthy when it comes to coupling. Contributing to the issue is that many women's perceptions have been thwarted regarding what qualities to look for in a man—what makes a man attractive. The media has sold us a lousy bag of goods in that department. The media's unrealistic portrayal of heroic guys who jump from building to building, or the sexy bad guys, has distorted what women should look for in men—and it has not provided good or realistic role models to men.

The kindest, best guys, who would make us women truly happy, are often overlooked in real life, because some of their finest inner qualities are seen as feminine and not presented in good light often enough in the stories we watch. A mentally, emotionally, spiritually healthy man would need to possess some feminine qualities, for a balanced yin and yang! With this distorted picture of what a man should be like, women can end up in very unsatisfactory relationships, where their needs are not being met, at best—at worst, they can find themselves in an abusive relationship.

When men are uncomfortable with a woman asking to be seen as equal to them, it is likely out of fear. To put some of those fears at ease, men need to understand that most of us women aren't asking for sameness. Men and women are gloriously different in ways we love. What women are asking for is the recognition of our equal human value. If some men are worried that a too confident, too independent partner will leave them, we can argue that a happy, respected, loved, and fulfilled woman is less likely to want to.

Equality for men and women is healthier for both parties. According to the *PLOS Global Public Health* gender study, when women are empowered, and we tackle long-standing gender inequality, we gain longevity! Equality extends our lives. Both genders benefit!

Yet, at this time, according to the WHO, and these are only reported cases, "nearly 1 in 3 women have been subjected to physical and/or sexual violence by an intimate partner or by non-partner sexual violence." A report by the UNODC states that as much as 58% of the murders of girls and women are committed by intimate partners or family members; after that comes stranger violence.

Young women attending college, working hard on their dreams and futures, are being sexually assaulted at an alarming rate, leaving these women shattered and changed. Some of these young women say they no longer feel at home in their own bodies; some drop out of school, derailing their future. For decades this has been swept under the rug by school officials.

Women have been set up and trained to compete with each other, which weakens us. For the longest time, women were to be homebound and dependent on their husbands without careers or a means of livable income of their own. Women weren't allowed to own property, make contracts, or vote. They needed a husband for a roof over their head, respect, stability, and for living in general. Undue pressure was put on women to find the guy with the money when the path to happiness would be finding a man capable of deep love. An atmosphere of competition was created among women.

A woman's appearance became disproportionately important. Magazines filled with airbrushed models created unrealistic standards for girls and women to compare themselves to and to make them "relationship-worthy." Men weren't under the same scrutiny. This created issues with self-esteem and self-love, causing further harm to women and girls. There's also a fear of aging for otherwise bright women with so much to offer the world. This fear has been instilled in women through the streams of films and TV shows, where unattractive or regular-looking men can be cast as leads at any age, but their girlfriends or wives must always be young and gorgeous. Women over 40 have a hard time finding work in leading roles in movies, especially romantic leading roles, which is not the case for men. This has created a bizarre onscreen world consisting of mostly young women. Some of the most incredible women are aged out and become nonexistent or demoted to background type of roles, in stories that are supposed to reflect life. Women are working to change this, and we are starting to see improvements onscreen.

Yet, just when we convince some of the advertisers to consider using regular-looking, real people type of models in their ads, AI's extreme beauty filters come along, destroying many women's ability to accept themselves once again. These severe filters are triggering new emotional and mental health issues for countless women. Men also get bamboozled into fantasizing about this fake beauty as being real, making it harder for them to appreciate and enjoy the genuine women in their lives, right in front of them.

It is wonderful that some women are starting to work in alliance with each other to make a positive difference in the world. We need to remember that when empowering ourselves, it is important that we have the courage to bring more of the healing *feminine* principles to the table and not just do what the men are doing in an effort to fit in.

Additionally, many women may see themselves as inclusive of other women but are not quite there yet. Women being supportive of other women means those outside of one's accepted "circle" too. It means being open, inclusive, and helpful—even to outside women whose personal power matches or exceeds one's own. Men have been outstanding collaborators, and they are running the world! May we women find it within ourselves to let go of the fears that have been instilled in us and vastly improve our collaboration skills. We could make incredible strides for humanity and the planet if we do!

Meanwhile, keep reading. What is going on for women is entwined with what is going on for men.

Effects of Removing Our Divine Mother on Men and Boys

It is not just women who have suffered the loss of their Divine Mother, since from that moment on we were taught not to fully value women and anything we feminize, which includes our emotions, sensitivity, compassion, and empathy. These are crucial parts of who we are, no matter our gender. We need these qualities in the right proportions to relate to ourselves and others; we need them for decision-making; we need them for mental, emotional, and spiritual health. Women haven't just lost their equal value as humans, becoming dangerously objectified, men have been left without the tools for their emotional and spiritual well-being.

A man chimed in at an author's event where we were talking about the issues women face and he said, "I'm so tired of hearing about all these injustices towards women! Well, guess what? Women aren't the only ones being victimized. Men suffer injustices too! We are considered unmanly if we cry or feel pain, for instance. We aren't allowed to express our emotions, and we can't show fear or ask for help without being ridiculed and emasculated!"

I felt this man's agony and empathized. I tried to explain that we were on the same page and talking about the same thing! The reason these healthy emotions aren't allowed in men is because they are associated with the feminine. What he is describing is the suppression and degradation of feminine qualities. Men ended up unintentionally damaged by this. Even women have been conditioned to see these healthy expressions, against our own best interest, as negative and unmasculine in men. For balance and wholeness, each gender must have some of the qualities of the other. Nothing on this planet is all male or all female—nothing and no one.

We are failing boys and men by the messages we inundate them with through the media, as well as at school and oftentimes at home. The messages of winning at all costs, the objectification of women, might is right, and man-up, puts a lot of pressure on our boys and young men who are in the process of developing and figuring out who they are. Early in life, boys show sensitivity and display healthy emotions. But then it is socialized out of them, or in some cases beaten out of them.

In the documentary *The Mask You Wear*, former NFL Coach Joe Herman says that most boys grow up hearing the harsh words "Be a man!" at some point in their lives. Herman says that these three words can be the most damaging words a boy can hear! The words come with the insinuation, that "a real man doesn't does not cry; a real man does not feel what you are feeling or do what you are doing. You need to stop and shut that down right now!" Because of this, too many men try not to show emotions, especially sorrow, fear, or hurt. If they do, they are a wimp, or, worse, acting like a girl. Boys who don't fit into this box are often bullied. We have it so backward. It takes trust, strength, and courage to show emotions and to talk about them!

With so much emotion denied or subjugated inside, mental illness can be triggered. Repressed emotions can also lead to escapism through drugs, and the suicide rate was higher in boys than girls for the longest time, though this is reversing, possibly due to the effects of the new social media pressures on girls. Men are also less likely to get help when their emotions are out of control because they fear that asking for help will make them look weak. Often asking for help doesn't even occur to them, it has been so conditioned out of them. With no place to go with their emotions, men are more prone to turn to outward displays of anger and aggression, which are sanctioned as masculine traits. Aggression without the feminine qualities of compassion and empathy to temper them, even towards oneself, can lead to a volatile situation. Repressed emotions can turn into explosive anger. In 90 % of homicides and 94 to 98% of mass shootings, the perpetrators are male. We need to stop right now and examine the messages we are sending our boys.

The other pressure on men has come about due to the time when women had so few rights, that they were utterly dependent on their husbands for any of life's necessities. Therefore, they needed to find prosperity via their partner. Currently, there is still undue pressure on men to be super successful so that they will be considered partnership-worthy by some women. Often men's self-esteem is tied up in this idea. Even wonderful men with a lovely home and family can see themselves as failures if they are not as financially successful as others. Many loving family guys don't have the drive or the willingness to forfeit time with their loved ones to put all their energy into climbing the corporate ladder. Think of George Bailey in the movie It's a Wonderful Life and his misperception of himself and all the value he brought to so many people's lives, due to what society deemed a successful man to look like.

To add to this, an outstanding young man I know recently expressed to me that he feels personally blamed for the patriarchal system everyone complains about, but which was manipulated into being thousands of years ago. The current generation of men was born into a system that came to feel normal but is unhealthy, though they aren't the ones responsible for creating it. The regular guys shouldn't be put in the same box as the Harvey Weinsteins. They are doing their best with what they know and are trying to come out from under what they have been taught by society and the media. He explained that there is a learning curve, so some patience is required. I agree. We are all learning as we go. Women and men need to take the time for healthy conversations where there is listening as well as talking. Neither party can come in, in a defensive mode or attack mode, and expect to be heard or expect to hear the information that may bring new understanding.

Even a positive transition will bring confusion. The depression rate has gone up. Part of it has to do with the uncertainty in the world with global warming, the division in our country, less personal human contact with automation and the internet, and so on. But even a positive transition to equality can bring utter confusion during the transition phase.

Exasperating the divide between men and women are the films and stories we watch and absorb daily. Films and video games highlight an aggressive, unrealistic, tough-guy, image for men. It's an action-packed masculinity, where men need to be invincible. Films don't show enough stories with a healthier, real-life representation of masculinity to balance out the fantasy representations. Even if we register this as unrealistic, coupled with the other messages men are getting, it is easy for a guy to feel inferior in comparison to this faux ideal and for women to be influenced by it as well.

What's most damaging is how often the cruel, bad guys are shown as the sexy ones, the ones who get all the women.

And usually, there is an additional message sent to men that one woman isn't enough. How messed up is that for both men and women to take in? Let's set this straight—the sexy bad guy image is a sham. When we are around someone with bad character, we notice pretty quickly that they make us miserable and sometimes unsafe. What is sexy is a wise, kind heart, and what generally brings happiness is a monogamous relationship built on love and trust.

The messages we get from religion, from society, and from the way women are depicted in film, TV shows, video games, and pornography—can create scenarios where violence against women is still all too common. Even the heroes in films are often shown as misogynistic. This needs to change, and filmmakers have that power. Again, it requires strength and courage to allow oneself to feel a full range of emotions and treat people right, especially anyone physically weaker than oneself. Jesus most certainly preached to treat "others", meaning everybody, all human beings with respect.

One of the darker consequences of the messages boys and men are getting in regard to women and girls come to our attention in the documentary, *The Hunting Ground*. It exposes the startling statistics about how frequently young women are raped by their male classmates while attending college. College should be a time for building on their dreams. Instead, in the blink of an eye, in many young women's lives, their capacity to feel at home in their own body anymore is destroyed without a second thought. These guys then continued to attend school, often sharing with friends and laughing about what happened. Many young women dropped out of college and some young women have taken their own lives, especially when they felt further violated after reporting the rape, by school officials sweeping the crime under the rug in favor of keeping their promising male athletes or students on the roster.

I remember many years ago, a co-worker shared that they had been awakened by the pounding on doors and cries for help in the halls of their apartment complex at 1:00 a.m., by a hysterical, terrified, naked, bloodied, teenaged girl, a young student. There was a college football party going on down the hall. This is what a gang rape looks like.! It is a violent act! The abysmal thing is that there did not appear to be ramifications for the male students who perpetrated this heinous act back then. I am tormented by this story and often wonder what happened to the young student after that. I tried to find out to no avail, since my co-worker, to my utter shock, said they did nothing to help her.

Many men don't fully grasp what a horrific act rape is. The rape culture grew because of the messages we are inundated with and because there were no real consequences for the guys who committed the acts—which further validated their view of women. Meanwhile, the young women's futures were derailed. This is changing now because parents, women, students, and some men have decided to take action. A judge was not too long ago recalled upon giving a male student what felt like a slap on the wrist after he sexually assaulted an unconscious female student. Those types of rapes have happened on campuses more than we would like to believe, and people are finally coming forward to put a stop to it. The young woman in this case was saved from further harm by two male students.

Though things are improving, the victim's statement shows that we still have a way to go when it comes to not victimizing the victim a second time in court. She described the court experience as harrowing. She said that instead of taking her time to heal, she was forced to recollect what happened in every tormenting detail in preparation for the defense attorney's manipulative questions. She felt she was being misled into undermining what she had said before and tricked out of her own self-worth.

Now that the male students are seeing serious consequences for their actions, these acts will more likely become a lot less frequent. But to avoid the derailing of young lives of either gender, we also need to stop the mentality behind it. We need to start nurturing and preserving the healthy emotional qualities our boys came in with at birth and have conversations at home and in school on the topic of honorable behavior and respect for girls and women. We can teach our boys the difference between assertiveness and aggression. More than anything, we need to lead by example.

There is a general assumption that the older generation of men would have even less regard for women than the younger generation, as we are influenced by the society around us. Some of that is true, but our individual wisdom, character, and heart come into play, too. It is not always generational, In the documentary, *Petals in the Dust*, about the dangers of being born female in India, it was the grandfather, the older man, who went to great lengths to find and save his newborn granddaughter when the father, his daughter's husband, tried to kill the little one for being born a female. Just imagine that for a moment. After frantically searching for a long time, the grandfather heard a faint cry and found her buried in a small ditch under layers of dirt. He cleared as much soil out of her mouth as he could and patiently, patiently massaged her, back to life.

Men are stepping forward to help. Rev. Matthew Fox has been leading talks on healing men and society through awareness and the embracing of the Sacred Masculine as opposed to the toxic masculine. What a gift. There have always been great men who exemplify this healthy masculinity. The two young men who came to the young woman's aide, for example. There have always been men who have gone against the status quo regarding how women were valued and treated before it even became popular. Jesus was one of them!

Hollywood has been a great problem with the blatant and covert messages it feeds to the world about women. Part of the issue is who is behind the camera. The Harvey Weinsteins have been painfully plentiful for centuries, especially in the film industry, doing much harm with the power they held. It wasn't just one guy. We can heal some of the pain caused by these men by specifically addressing the offenses and the offenders. A tiny handful of these offenders are now being called out through efforts such as the "Me Too Movement" and this is making some men nervous about their past behavior; many speak up against the movement, but how else will things change?

It's not just women taking a stand. There have always been men—even in Hollywood, who stand up for what's right. Decades ago, I remember working on a film where a man on the set intimidatingly pressed his hotel key in my hand and let me know to be in his room that evening. I said no to the proposition. He told me not to act like a child, if I wanted to make it in the film industry. I kept declining, but I was becoming shaken because he would not relent. I was trapped on the set with nowhere to go. The director saw what was happening, pulled me aside, and told me that his

11-year-old son had joined him on this trip and was in the end trailer, playing solitaire. He said that the boy would be happy for the company, and I would be safe there until they called me for the next scene. You cannot imagine the gratitude and sense of relief I felt. There are many men who have stayed solid no matter the environment they are surrounded by, and those who haven't always have the potential to grow.

Equality benefits all. When we all have equal human value, we live with mutual respect, mutual kindness, and mutual support on a human and spiritual level. There is a mutual sharing of each other's gifts and wisdom, both to solve the world's problems and benefit our lives. A study cited in the *Psychology Today* article, "Gender Equality Improves Life for Everyone", confirms that equality and a world where everyone can contribute and flourish, exponentially enhances everyone's happiness level and quality of life!

If you are a man reading this and you have in the past bought into some of the propaganda that puts down the women who ask for equality—or if you desire a deeper understanding regarding what women seek to heal, let's use our imagination to step into a woman's shoes. Close your eyes—now imagine if God was only spoken of as female; Mother God, Mother Holy Spirit, and a Divine Daughter, all make up the Trinity that you will live with your whole life. There used to be a Father God, but he was removed and replaced with the feminine thousands of years ago and humanity since then has not known any masculine aspect to God. God is female only. Imagine when we talk about all of humanity, we call it woman or womankind, as opposed to man/mankind. With these changes, you will start seeing less of your reflection everywhere. The same opportunities women have, are not afforded to you. The God-given gifts you come in with you also leave with. Your talents have gone to waste because the doors are simply shut that would have allowed you to use them. Imagine doing the same job but getting paid less than a woman does, which means you can afford less than the woman does. Only women get all the positions of power that affect the world; only women tell the stories and make the movies that show only our perception of the world. Even men's stories are told by women. Imagine everything that has to do with men and the masculine as having less value, getting less respect, and not being taken as seriously, no matter how much you have to contribute and no matter how hard you protest that this simply isn't right. Imagine these things, then go back and combine them with the dangers and other things we discussed in the "Effects on Women and Girls" section.

No one would want these circumstances for themselves. Yet feminism has been framed to look like a harsh response to life by angry women, but it is the blocking and resistance to reasonable requests for equality as humans that create the harm and problems. There is a lot of click-bait type of misinformation about what the women's movement stands for being presented to men on the internet, especially to young men, by those who don't want things to change. To make things more complicated, there will always be a few women whose actions don't represent the heart of the movement. Most in the feminist movement, whether female or male, are asking to be heard and understood when asking for equality and fairness for women. This will not only benefit women; it will benefit men and the planet as well. They are asking for a necessary change.

John 13:34

> A new commandment I give unto you: That you love one another, as I have loved you, that you also love one another.

Effects of Removing Our Divine Mother on Marriage and Relationships

During this time of transition towards gender equality, dating and relationships can be more challenging. As mentioned, there tends to be confusion as we struggle to find new ways to relate with each other. Anytime we transition from one set of principles to another, even if we are on a path to a healthier blend of energies, we can expect a certain amount of chaos.

Women who used to depend on men to live, now have more options. Yet, women are still fighting for true equality. This is can be overwhelming, as women do not feel that they are on stable ground yet and many women are justifiably angry about what they have dealt with. On the other hand, many men are unclear about what is expected of them as the changes take place and are sincerely doing their best. We need to be careful not to make each other the enemy.

One of my main goals with this book is to bring our Divine Mother back into our consciousness, healing our relationship with God and all there is. Accomplishing this involves another focus of mine and that is equality for women and girls. A fair society is required for global health. We can then relate in deeper more satisfying ways.

People aren't meant to be solitary creatures. Our mental and physical health are increased when we have a caring circle of friends and family around us. Therefore, we need to be watchful not to misdirect our anger. Much of our soul growth happens through relating. As far as romantic relationships go, this transitional period can be difficult, yet it can also bring us an opportunity to learn healthier ways of relating to each other.

It is more vital than ever for two people who are interested in each other to have conversations about what is important to them—and not only via text. Honest, heartfelt conversations, where each person shares and then truly listens to understand what the other person is feeling, are essential as we move forward.

Alas, our addiction to cell phones and social media is making relating and authentic communication difficult. We are so removed from each other. We even have a thing called "ghosting" now, where someone lacks the simple kindness to let the person they are conversing with know that they have changed their mind about them. This is not principled behavior. I'm disturbed by the stories I've heard from my young acting students who are dating. They describe cruel and discourteous behavior. It is sad to see the changes in character the internet has brought about. If we are aware of it, we can change it. We want to make sure that we are one of the people who treat others the way we would like to be treated. This very basic principle needs to be brought back, especially to the internet where people hurt other people while hiding behind the screen.

The confusion we are experiencing is not only regarding gender roles, relationships, and relating via the internet. There is great uncertainty regarding the health of society and the planet! The lack of stability in the world can affect our relationships. The practice of mindfulness can help ground us during these uncertain times; the importance of this cannot be overstated.

With the removal of the Divine Relationship between our Godly Mother and Godly Father, coupled with the damaging account of Adam and Eve, we have been living with a wounded understanding of what relationships are all about. The deep comradery and unifying passion of equals that was given to us at the beginning of Genesis 1 was damaged.

When Augustine's spin on the Adam and Eve story took hold, our equal value as humans was thrown further off balance. Sex became shameful and sinful, placing yet another wedge between us and our ability to experience true intimacy. Now society has rebelled and is turning having sex into something trivial, which, again, is an obstacle to true intimacy. Sex is neither sinful nor trivial. The transformational mind, body, spirit bond we were meant to relish comes from deep, meaningful intimacy in an equal relationship.

In any relationship, especially in a committed relationship such as a marriage, inequality doesn't bring out the best in either party. When one party is not being heard, valued, or entirely respected, it is difficult to get close. Fear can create the need to control another person. The person being controlled and not fully valued feels resentment that may come out in seemingly unrelated arguments. An unfulfilled person has less to bring to a partnership, so both people miss out. The person under someone else's control, with fewer rights and opportunities, is often put in the position of having to use covert means to get some of their needs and wants met. I remember many of the old TV comedies showing wives sneakily finding ways to get their husbands to do what they wanted. They saw it as their only option. This makes for great comedy, but it does not make for a healthy relationship. As mentioned, the study published in the journal PLOS Global Public Health reveals that people of both genders live longer and are happier in countries where there is more gender equality. They enjoy each other better. Quality of life and quality of relationships are closely related.

We have already discussed the devastating ramifications for women in abusive relationships. In this section, we examine how society's undervaluing of women can subtly affect even our most typical relationships in seemingly small ways. All of us can pick up behaviors without realizing it. One common issue has to do with time perception and respect for time spent. In general, men's time is seen as more valuable and limited, and women's time is seen as less valuable and somehow unlimited. In that mindset, it's okay to put all the things one doesn't want to do on woman's plate. This misperception comes from the degradation of the feminine. We have subliminally been taught to not fully respect, or take as seriously, the attributes and skills women bring to the table. This can even happen in an otherwise loving home.

A typical example is when a wife's career has less perceived value than a husband's. This makes it so that even with rising equality, women who work outside the home still are expected to carry the brunt of the household responsibilities on their shoulders once they get home, rather than being more evenly split. Even many stay-at-home moms with several kids to care for juggle so many different duties that they are constantly working overtime. Yet their time spent working somehow has less value than their husband's, despite the crucial work they are doing. This means that career women and many stay-at-home moms have far less time for themselves and for doing something they love, compared to their male counterparts. This depletes the female spirit.

The results from an *Office for National Statistics Report* in the UK show that men get about 5 hours more time for leisure activities per week than their wives. This is a huge difference! For women, there is no real time to regenerate! Women not having enough time for recouping and for fun has nothing to do with women not organizing their time better. There are only so many hours in a day.

Part of what makes it so difficult for women to take time for themselves and decompress, is the unfair distribution of unpaid work, or what is better described as "invisible labor." What amplifies this situation is if, for example, a wife spends hours cleaning the house only for their mate to come home in the evening, and without thinking, undo the work by throwing down their things, eating, leaving out dishes, garbage, etc. The wife is made to look like a petty nag if she continually speaks up. Why can't she just let him be? If this same wife, however, went to her husband's office and deleted 5 or more hours of work off his computer, he would think that she had lost her mind and would be outraged, not recognizing the same exhausted exasperation in his wife's eyes. He doesn't see what he is doing as impacting her workload in the same light and that he is affecting the amount of time she will have for herself at the end of the day.

He doesn't see how this slowly chips away at their marriage and trust because it is clear to his wife that it is a matter of him not caring enough about what matters to her and what hurts her. To him, he sees it as silly to get upset about—which is a matter of not giving her time and the work she does enough value. A husband can shut his door at work, come home and relax. For the wife, home is where she works and it affects her mental, emotional, and spiritual health if she can't decompress because she needs to be worried that the tasks she accomplished will not remain off her plate.

Wives and mothers can't close that office door and be done for the day. There are constant needs, especially with children, who can be unpredictable and will keep a mother plenty busy. A mother is always surrounded by her work, and there is always something that needs to be done to prepare for the next day. Imagine the reduction in stress and anxiety she would experience if she knew she could trust that her partner had her back and wouldn't undo what she had finished.

Recently, by chance, I came across an article in *The Atlantic,* written by a man, Matthew Fray, titled, "The Marriage Lesson I Learned Too Late." I had never seen an article like this coming from a man's heartfelt perspective on this topic. The link to his story is cited in the back of the book. Matthew Fray shared how never honoring his wife's requests to respect her time and for him to not undo what she accomplished by thoughtlessly creating additional work for her at home; something that felt trivial to him—corroded his wife's feelings for him over time and eventually ended their marriage. It was heartbreaking that he hadn't realized it sooner. He was sincere in his reflections now.

Conversely, I knew a young couple years ago who had the most loving and mutually respectful relationship I had seen. Not surprisingly, the pair both came from homes where their parents modeled that behavior in their relationship. What I noticed in this young couple was a love with a deep concern and respect for the other person's feelings and an attitude of gratitude for each other.

This book is focused on healing the feminine, so we can't get into the many dynamics of a loving relationship. There are wonderful books available to us that go into depth on that topic. I do want to take a moment to mention how vital it is that **both** partners regard the well-being of the other. It is a two-way street, and it truly starts with the seemingly little things.

In Arthur Brooks' well-researched article, "The Type of Love That Makes People Happiest," he discloses that for a genuinely happy, lasting, romantic relationship, friendship is more important than anything else. Passion is fantastic, especially in the beginning—but lifelong happiness depends on relationship satisfaction, which depends on what Arthur refers to as "companionate love." He describes companionate love as being less based over time on the crazy, passionate rollercoaster highs and lows of new love, but rather "more on a stable affection and love, with mutual understanding, and commitment." This is not as unexciting as it may sound—to the contrary. Rather than being in a marriage to raise kids or to have financial security, or strictly looking for those fleeting highs, in this type of relationship there is camaraderie and genuine joy in being together. It's based on common interests, equality, thoughtfulness, affection, friendship—where each person has the other's back and truly cares about their partner's feelings and well-being. Sex becomes pleasantly satisfactory, and Arthur states the happiest relationships are monogamous.

This reminds me of the long marriage of a distant, older relative of mine. As a young child I couldn't help but notice how much genuine fun they had together. I noticed their mutual care, respect, and how they got along. There was always so much laughter between the two of them. Decades went by. I ran into the wife shortly after her husband had passed away. We stood there talking. I said how sorry I was for her loss. She looked at me thoughtfully and said, "Fifty years together and still not long enough!" That is the kind of genuine love and partnership most of us wish for, where no matter how long we have been together, we would do anything for just one more day with that person.

Effects of Removing Our Divine Mother on Diversity of All Kinds

Paul said in Galatians 3:28:

> "There is neither Jew nor Greek: there is neither bond nor free: there is neither male nor female. For you are **all** one in Christ Jesus."

The above quote shares one of Jesus' main messages. Yet, our fractured divine family has impaired our ability to recognize our global family in humanity. We instead have a fear of the other—anyone different from us is a threat. Humanity has done much harm out of fear. We have exacted this damage in our personal and intimate relationships, and we have done so in the religious, political, economic global arena. We can be sure that much of what transpired during the editing of our Bible regarding women was done out of fear. People only try to diminish and control what they fear. There would be no need to expend the time and energy otherwise.

In the world where our Divine Mother's compassion and unconditional love were rejected now lives a fear of people of other religions, races, cultures, gender identities, and sexualities. We see strangers as our enemies, instead of the incredible human beings, brothers or sisters that we haven't gotten to know yet. There is diversity in God's design.

Instead of focusing on our commonalities and our shared humanity, there's a fear of lack—a fear that there isn't enough to go around, and a negative focus on our differences. There's a fear of connection, not realizing that all is already beautifully interconnected in every way. What we do to one another, good or bad, will come back to us because of this connection. Our own lives would improve exponentially if we treated each other better and celebrated diversity.

Watching TV now, I appreciate the diversity in the characters appearing on screen; this will help shift people's perspectives. With familiarity, the angst will dissipate. Media has power and we weren't exposed to diversity in our daily stories for the first 100 years. People of color in movies and TV shows were a rarity. The absence of people of color on screen gave the false sense they were not living or contributing to society as fully, or that they were some-how on the fringe and not "like us". White people played the parts of Native Americans. Destructive stereotypes further perpetuated feelings of fear and alienation. We rarely saw people of diverse sexual orientations or gender identities. And it's not that there weren't gay people in Hollywood. But they had to hide their sexuality from the world for fear of loss of livelihood, loss of friends, or loss of life. There are still risks. This is only beginning to be healed; we are not there yet. Conscious films help us understand each other. God made us equal but with joyful variety.

Romans 1:26-27 has been used to prove that homosex-uality is condemned in the Bible. This doesn't seem to be accurate. Discussions about homosexuality aren't found in the Bible, except very briefly in Romans and Corinthians. And here, many scholars claim that, with concise transla-tion, what is being condemned is pederasty, prostitution, and rape in the context of homosexual relationships. Loving, committed same-sex relationships aren't a topic in the Bible. Ally Kateusz shares that sanctioned same sex mar-ried couples are depicted respectfully on ancient catacomb sarcophagi. Who suddenly made this type of love wrong?

We all have biases that were formed over our lifetime that would be beneficial to clear. These biases were fed to us through the media, by the people around us, and by the things we experienced. It is important to take the time to lay them bare—so we can understand and heal them.

I started the Conscious Media Movement because stories and film, when used wisely, can be powerful tools to help us walk in someone else's shoes. The saying that no one is equal until we are all equal is so true. We are all in the same boat, struggling with similar feelings. We all long to love and be loved. We all long to be heard and understood. We all want to matter. Conscious living would wake us up to celebrate our vast diversity as well as our common humanity, by bringing the heart-centered, compassionate, feminine perspective into our consciousness and lives. Mindfulness practices, good films, good books, and traveling to foreign lands, all open our minds and hearts to others.

Recently, I heard about the most amazing libraries scattered all over the world—called Human Libraries! Their purpose is to challenge stereotypes and prejudices through dialogue! Here, people are the books who go on loan to us to chat with and ask questions of! How amazing! The idea is, that if there is a type of person that we feel uncomfortable around, fear, or simply don't understand—such as someone of a different race, gender identity, or religion, we can ask to meet them and speak face-to-face to gain a new perspective! These courageous people are kind to help others in this manner! It's a heart-centered approach that lifts the veil so that we can learn about one another, feel our humanness, release misconceptions, and start enjoying each other. Such a brilliant idea! Look into it. There may be such a library near you!

The Effects of Removing Our Divine Mother on Nature and Climate Change

We were named the stewards, the caretakers of our precious Mother Earth. Instead of caretaking, we exploited and ravished her. The effects of removing Mother God from our world have been devastating for the health of our planet. Many feel it's too late to turn things around. No one is listening or doing enough fast enough. I feel the urgency too. I've also noticed that there is something vital we are overlooking altogether. As long as we view climate change as a strictly physical problem, our planet will not survive—as it is also a deeply rooted spiritual one. We lost the nurturing heart and soul of the cosmos, and she needs to be brought back to allow for a healing of enormous proportions.

We have missed the boat when it comes to saving ourselves by physical means alone. While we do need to take immediate physical action, simultaneously we need to start raising mass consciousness so we can get ourselves onto the path of spiritual healing. We need to not only look at the physical but also at the metaphysical and the spiritual. The universe is not flat. It is multidimensional, and we can engage with it at a deeper level through meditation and through our relationship with nature.

Nature has always been associated with the feminine. With the portrayal of men dominating women in the Bible, that assumed right extended itself to trying to dominate nature as well, instead of respectfully and joyfully living in harmony with her.

How many of us take the time to go outside regularly and drink in its awe-inspiring beauty? We are nature. Nature is not separate from us. It is who we are. If we understood that, we would treat all of life differently. We would do everything possible to bring the equilibrium back. We are not here alone. The lives of the creatures around us are not insignificant and everything we do has a domino effect. If we poison the rat, we not only inhumanely kill the rat, but we may also end up killing a hawk or owl that eats the rat, or your family cat. Live traps used with peanut butter work well. I can attest to that. I used one when roof rats drifted into our area. I checked the trap daily. It took just a few days. I then let the cute, little fellow free in a wooded area not more than a mile from where I found it, so it could find its way back to their family. Then I made sure to immediately locate and cover the hole the rat found access through. There were no more problems after that, and no chain of animals were harmed.

We are part of an intricate, interwoven ecosystem. When that is thrown off enough, everything goes. Do we grasp what is at stake? I shared about the spiritual beauty of nature in my Conscious Media Movement blog years ago. I wrote:

> "Spending even as little as a few minutes
> in nature already creates a healing shift in
> our body, heart, and soul. Lay on the grass
> under a tree and just watch and listen. You
> suddenly notice birds looking for food, bugs
> flying by, plants, trees—a worm digging a
> tunnel, a squirrel storing nuts for the winter.
> There are billions and billions of creatures
> living on this planet at the same time as us.
> There's a vast ocean of life, the skies and
> the earth all filled with living beings going

about their day. Suddenly the little capsule
of thought playing around in our head can
finally burst open and our own personal
problems appear smaller when we realize
that there is so much life going on besides
just us and our small circle."

Let's get out of our heads and back into our Mother's
heart. Stop seeing ourselves so separate from our neighbors
or people of different genders, religions, cultures, and all of
the nature beings. At some point, we forgot that the whole
Cosmos is a living entity with a consciousness we are all part
of and partake in together. Men and women must connect
to the feminine soul of the cosmos again, for inspiration in
what to do next.

Baby steps won't do, or we will all die. There needs to be
a serious paradigm shift and a new way of doing things—**a
new way of living**. We are destroying the very system we
are entirely dependent upon. Humanity must organize at a
global level to scale down and, where possible, phase out
such things as fossil fuel extraction, deforestation, indus-
trial pollution, etc. And we must also do our part at home.

Science backs that the early indicators of climate change
we are already experiencing in the world are increasing. At
first, there will be gradual changes in far off places, giving
us the false hope that we can take our time with small,
incremental improvements. Yet, we too are already experiencing some of these changes, with fires, floods, hazardous
air quality alerts, and unusual weather. The slower pace
will not continue for long. What happens in the Antarctic,
or anywhere, for that matter, will affect the entire planet.
The dominos are being set up folks, while we are too busy

going about our daily tasks to notice. And when these shifts in temperature hit a certain point, the speed of the disasters happening will be like a light switch was turned on. These catastrophes will come at unspeakable magnitude and be unstoppable at that point. Our young adults and children on our planet right now will highly likely be here when this happens. Who has the kind of conscience that is fine with doing nothing to stop it? That is our fate and our children's fate unless we take dramatic, immediate, new action. We can't keep trying to fix things with the thinking and the methods that haven't brought solutions. The complete shift in priorities and choices required from all of us will at first seem shocking and take us out of our comfort zones. After deep reflection and meditation, the new direction we need to go will suddenly make complete sense. More on this later.

It will be challenging to change what the biggest polluters are doing. After years of stalling the process, multiple lawsuits are now being brought against the oil companies for deceiving and failing to warn the public about the dangers of fossil fuels to our climate. According to the charges filed, these companies knew the catastrophe they were creating for the planet, as they made away with trillions of dollars in profits. These lawsuits could create hopeful changes.

According to the new study just published in the journal "PLOS Climate," 10% of the richest people in America are responsible for almost half (about 40%) of the planet-heating pollution! The biggest offenders are those at the very top with their much-used private jets that emit tons of carbon pollution, their colossal homes, and the companies they invest in. The super-emitters, who are among the top .1%, produce around 3,000 tons of carbon pollution per year! These lifestyles can make it impossible for us to reach our sustainable planet goals. This is what the lawsuits are at least partially addressing. It is good to be aware of what we are dealing with here.

We will want to continue to do our part at home while, also becoming more involved in what is happening in the world. Jason Hickel of the *Correspondent* in his article, "Jason Hickel: Outgrowing Growth: Why Quality of Life, Not GDP, Should Be Our Measure of Success," says that something big needs to happen on the climate scene. Already several years ago, scientists at the Stockholm Environment Institute estimated that the biggest polluters, North America, and some European countries, need to reach net zero in emissions before 2030. Hickel says we are too relaxed about reaching this goal. After over 250 years of creating a global fossil fuel infrastructure, we may not realize the intense healing curve. The rest of the world has only a little longer. Meeting this goal requires immediate drastic action, but again, we are not seeing nearly enough of it. We keep missing our deadlines. It will take **all** of us to make enough of a difference. More activists are needed. May we educate ourselves and find what area of climate change or social change we can dedicate time to.

One of the issues we can all do something about is consumerism, through a radical change in mindset! We are sacrificing our planet, the nature beings on it, and our own lives—for things—lots and lots of manufactured stupid things we don't even need. This addiction to things we don't need will contribute to the death of us. More on consumerism later in this book.

Meanwhile, imagine the simple lifestyles back in the days of the pioneers—how little they needed to get by. I am not suggesting going back to those living conditions, but it

is worth pointing out how liberating it is to purge and sim-
plify our living space and lives of too much stuff. Nature
was all around people back then, friends visited up close
and personal, and there wasn't a need for the trillions of
things we buy. We need to come out from under the spell
put over us by the advertisers making us believe we need it
need it all; these things that distract us and wreak havoc on
our environment. To get out from under that spell would be
freedom! Freedom to put our attention to what matters most
in life—our self-development, our family, our relationships,
our goals, and dreams, making memories, connecting with
nature, connecting to others, and connecting to God.

Though we have used our lands for farming food in
the past, the manner in which we farm has changed. It has
become a monoculture industry. Rather than the diverse
crops the farmers of old used to grow, there is a factory farm
system in place that strips and deadens the soils and con-
taminates our water and air. It kills pollinating insects and
attracts disease. An ultimatum for changing this destructive
system to one of restorative agriculture is a must, coupled
with the governments aiding the farms with their transition, as it will require time and money.

These conscious farming methods work in sync with
nature. Restorative agriculture replenishes the soil. Done
right, it can improve entire ecosystems! The destructiveness
is not necessary!

May we passionately protect our open spaces and
national parks. We are in great danger of losing what can't
be replaced. Designated land must be safeguarded. Once our
open spaces and parks are gone, there is no turning back.
We have the moral duty to move from a humanity based on
collecting wealth and material things to a humanity valuing

life. May we become a humanity with life-sustaining principles and values, working in harmony with the environment that sustains us.

We need to bring more nature into our cities. More carbon sequestering trees in our cities would improve air quality and provide the tranquility that even a small slice of nature brings. There is a direct association with more nature areas in cities and improved mental health and lower crime rates.

Instead of focusing on our differences, can we focus on common goals? Let's get to know our neighbors better and build a sense of community again. We can organize meetups and start supporting each other to move towards green living. I have seen this done in a California town. It needs to spread. Discuss green living, composting, commuting, and cleaner energy options. Solar has become affordable and advantageous. Set up a neighborhood trade and swap. The community can also "adopt" a business or corporation they set out to transform.

As mentioned, corporations, including "Big Oil" have been given a license to destroy the planet, and they are doing so at record speed. Our governments have allowed this to happen! No more! We have been bamboozled and lied to in so many ways. It's time to take our power back. It is our current, capitalistic economic system that is by far doing the most cataclysmic harm to our planet—this has created an unsustainable way of life we are all stuck in. But we can wake up and make the needed changes.

Anne Baring has spoken on the topic, pointing out that, "we live in a world that has been governed by the masculine archetype for some 4,000 years, with no feminine archetype to balance it, no sacred marriage between them. As a result, world culture and the human psyche have become dangerously out of balance, out of alignment with the Earth and the Cosmos."

Anne further explains that "through the eyes and heart of the mother, we get a completely different perspective on life...a perspective which recognizes that we live on a sacred planet; that our lives participate in a Sacred Cosmic Order and that our role as humans is to care for the life of this planet. The feminine stands for the soul, for the heart, and for compassion and justice...the two primary values which protect and serve life."

Until we bring back the missing part of the cosmos and all the loving, restorative qualities and wisdom that come with her, we will futilely be patching up holes rather than healing the whole. I write this to motivate us! A vital shift in consciousness is essential. We need to look at our planet differently. Nature has been waiting for us to work with her so she can be restored. She's on our side, but there will be a tipping point. For humanity to survive, something new needs to be implemented, a culture of harmonious collaboration with nature and each other that comes from acknowledging our connectedness!

Effects of Removing Our Divine Mother on Film and Story

What we watch every day in films and the media has an enormous effect on society. Stories influence the way we think and can teach us healthy or destructive behaviors that we come to accept as normal. What we watch and absorb daily affects our psyche, our emotional, spiritual health, and our lens of perception, as much as what we eat every day affects our body and physical health! Much of what we have been absorbing through the media is destructive and does not come from our higher conscious expressions. The world needs more conscious filmmakers to help uplift society!

The gender imbalance in society has been kept alive by what we are seeing and "learning" from the shows and films we view. For over a century, they have been directed primarily by one gender only! The effect of removing our Divine Mother from the picture is amplified in the film business. For over 100 years, about 96% of what we have watched and learned about life from, including the chick flicks or "women's films," have been directed by men, providing almost an entirely male perspective to life! And this is not because there weren't or aren't enough gifted, qualified women directors pounding on the door trying to break in. There have been a rare few women directors hired on studio films in the past, before our recent breakthroughs for women, but when that happened, there were countless other stressful challenges and serious obstacles presented to those women that men didn't deal with—before, during, and after production. Women directors also seem to need to be twice as good to get half the positive reviews. The percentage of women directors put on studio films was increasing in tiny increments only, and at one point made it to 11%. However, with filmmaker Greta Gerwig breaking box office records, we hopefully will see slightly faster improvements for women directors now. Though, it doesn't look like we will hit the fifty percent mark any time soon.

Also, the vast collection of films we have accumulated from the past century are all primarily directed by men, and these films, these stories, will continue to influence society. It's simply been a man's world behind the camera, where the films get made and the stories get told.

In front of the camera, it was only slightly better for women, though it was far from equal in pay, screen time, parts, and quality opportunities. Before Geena Davis founded the Geena Davis Institute to advocate for healthier representation for women and girls in films, the ratio was 2.42 males to 1 female cast in films, even though, women make up slightly over 50% of the population! There was this world created on the screen, where women simply didn't exist as much. Even the crowd scenes were comprised of about 70% men.

I remember seeing a pie chart of leading film role distribution in the early 1980s. If my memory serves me right, it was around 70% of leading roles that went to men and the rest were split between women and children. If you were a woman of color, the odds were even worse. What a warped worldview this presented.

Strides have been made these past 18 years, and we have Geena Davis to thank for that. Since she started the Geena Davis Institute in 2004, we have started to see a shift in the quality and number of interesting parts for women and girls—but we still have a long way to go. As we get more women behind the camera, we will see further progress in front of the camera.

How women are portrayed in films affects how they are seen in the world. When it is one gender running the show, or better said, running the world, there are automatically biases built into everything, even if unintentional. Especially in the past, women's characters were often one-dimensional or misrepresented. So many times, I watched a movie where I thought, "Wow, I don't know too many women who would react that way in that situation. Who is making this stuff up?" Often women were cast only as eye-candy. Most women characters weren't named. In the few conversations women had in films, they were usually talking about men. Though there were rare exceptions, most of the time the token actress cast in a film was the male lead character's girlfriend or wife, and rarely were they the problem solvers, the ones doing exciting things, or the ones who moved the plot forward. Young girls were sexualized at an early age.

It isn't as bad now as it was back then, yet these stereotypes are still found in films and shows produced today. They send a terrible message to women and girls that they have limited capabilities and value. It also sends that same message to boys. We continue to push for this to change. Filmmakers also need to be careful when trying to present a strong woman, to not only show strength in masculine terms. The feminine has incredible strengths of its own.

I also noticed that in family films of the past, the mother had often died or ran off, with the latter being especially contrary to real life. This was likely not done with ill intent but rather because most male directors had a hard time getting into a woman's head and therefore didn't want to deal with trying to develop a complex female character. It was easier to write the woman out of the story. Instead, they put a man in the part of a single parent, despite the fact that during those times especially, it was by a landslide the mothers who were raising the kids on their own. Yet, they found no support in the stories they watched. These brave, hardworking women usually lived on low incomes, juggling much and struggling to make ends meet—and equal pay was not a real part of the conversation yet. Single moms had a big disadvantage when it came to financial quality of life, which affected many other things. When these tired, single moms went to watch a movie with their kids, they were greeted by a faux world of charming hero, single dads on the screens.

Most lead actresses are being paid a fraction of their male counterpart's rate, even when the actress is a top-billed talent. I recall the early trailblazer actress Suzanne Sommers saying that she was fired for asking for equal pay when her contract came up to be renegotiated for her role as Chrissy in *Three is Company.* She said in one interview that men in film and television were being paid 5 to 10 times as much as their female costars. The higher dollar amounts Hollywood deals with help to bring attention to what is happening for most women in the workforce in less noticeable ways. Though we are dealing with lower paychecks, the discrepancies greatly affect what women, versus what men are able to do with their lives.

According to a *USA Today* article, when reshoots were required for the film, *All the Money in the World,* Michelle Williams, the top-billed star, who was later nominated for a Golden Globe Award for her performance in that film made less than one-tenth of 1% of what Mark Wahlberg was purportedly paid! She got under $1,000 for the shoot via per diems and Wahlberg got $1.5 million. What makes it more disturbing is that according to what I read in other articles, they both had the same agent negotiating their contracts. Williams was said to have been "paralyzed" when she found out about the huge discrepancy and is now at the forefront of fighting for equal pay. I included links to articles regarding what happened in the reference section. (Wahlberg later donated the money he got when everything came to light).

It is ironic that the idea to use moving pictures to tell a story came from a woman, Alice Guy-Blaché! A man, Louis Lumière, invented the cinematographe in 1895 which was mainly used for demonstrations and to sell cameras. Alice Guy-Blaché is believed to be the very first to have the idea of using the medium to tell a fictional story. Though some dispute her being the first, most historians maintain Alice Guy's claim that her story film, *The Cabbage Fairy*, in 1896 came before the story films of Georges Méliès. She had the idea. *The Cabbage Fairy* is considered to be the first scripted narrative film ever made! Alice went on to make hundreds of other films. Yet, she was erased from film history when the industry became powerfully male-dominated, and many of her films became wrongly credited to a male colleague—a pattern we see time and time again.

Geena Davis has made a positive change as far as the quality of the roles in front of the camera for women, girls, and minorities. As far as the position of director goes, the lead person with the power to tell the stories, the pie chart still looks bad. For ages, only about 4% of those hired by studios to direct a film were women. For well over a century, we have been seeing the world and learning what to accept exclusively through men's eyes. Even stories written by women have the male director's distinct spin on them. The experiences of women, the experiences of mothers, are not told through a woman's heart, with her wisdom, not even in children's films! What a loss to humanity!

The female voice is gaining strength in the entertainment industry, and this will support the rise of the Divine Feminine into the world. Taylor Swift is at the forefront of this shift. She was named "Person of the Year" in 2023 and graced the cover of *Time*, a huge breakthrough for a woman, and especially for someone so young. Let's remember that the franchise used to be called "Man of the Year" until 1999, and mostly featured male leaders of countries or corporations.

Swift has courageously broken through major barriers for herself and women. She also makes the effort to give back to society. According to Sam Jacob's *Time* article, "The Choice", Swift has overcome colossal obstacles and setbacks put in her path while making her dreams happen, becoming "both the writer and hero of her own story". I love the sound of that! No wonder she has become an inspiration to so many women and girls! She is ushering in a time when we too can become the writers and heroes of our own stories and contribute our God-given gifts to humanity!

Consciousness matters! I founded the Conscious Media Movement some years ago to urge filmmakers and producers of all genres to create stories that raise our consciousness and with that help to heal humanity and the planet. What we absorb day in and day out has a tremendous effect on our psyche. Films can influence society; this influence has been wasted and abused. The power of film was misused for war propaganda films, and in our everyday films and TV shows, far too many are produced thoughtlessly or for shock value rather than actual value. Even some supposed anti-war films we have watched, subliminally slip in messages meant to thoroughly dehumanize the other.

Conscious films are harder to write and produce, with the biggest challenge being that the filmmaker needs to be rid of their prejudices and hate and be wise and highly conscious themselves to produce media that both entertains and raises consciousness! There are no shortcuts! They need to have done their inner work, to work from the heart. When we peruse the vast selection of mind-numbing or worse films and shows, we can see that we have incredibly far to go in that department. Even some current, popular films that are intended to be conscious media can have destructive elements mixed in with the good, due to where the filmmaker is still at in their development. If they lack true wisdom, we can end up with faux-conscious media.

With that in mind, the Conscious Media Movement will include a platform where filmmakers, who desire to be among the changemakers, can go for support on their spiritual journeys. The first step is to commit to living more mindfully in our everyday lives, the next step is to find a spiritual practice we connect to and will practice consistently. Embarking on this journey is both exciting and challenging. Therefore, it helps to have a support system, though it is also a private, personal journey.

Read about what is happening in the world and what more conscious organizations such as some of the ones mentioned in the back of this book are doing. We need to do a combination of spiritual practice, conscious living, and research. This is the only way we can elevate our consciousness to tell the kind of stories that will help humanity.

Filmmakers have the tools to make an enormous difference. With so much destructive media out there, we can create an evolutionary shift for society by purposefully using story for good. We are not just talking about documentaries, which are powerful, but tend to attract people already seeking. Conscious media needs to be included in **all genres** for it to reach people from all walks of life. Tidbits of consciousness raising information can even be added to a finished screenplay or book in the little daily actions our characters undertake.

Stay aware of the misinformation and corruption we are exposed to in the world. We need to be incredibly sagacious. Explore multiple opposing media sources. We don't want to get all of our information from just one source to understand where other people are coming from. Much supposed information is "funded" by special interests. All the division in our country and around the world has been orchestrated. We are all in what is happening on our planet together, and only together can we hope to save ourselves in time. Filmmakers can help heal the great divide.

I was profoundly moved by the satirical film *Don't Look Up!*, which calls out the misinformation and absurdities in our society; this is no matter what party. The film takes place in a fictional setting, with some dark humor thrown in. It is a commentary on the corruption in politics, and our inability to face reality and work together. Every genre lends itself to adding this type of cognizant wisdom to a story. We can expand people's awareness and encourage changes in habits and behaviors that will help to restore society and heal the planet.

Parents, we live in a media-saturated world. It is overwhelming and we may not be paying enough attention to what our children are watching. At a time when the media is being used to manipulate us to make choices against our best interests, it is extra important to pay attention to what our children and teens are absorbing on a daily basis. Please take the time to screen the media your young children are watching and take the time for discussions with your teens. Remember to listen.

We have discovered that the violence children watch on television increases risks of violent behavior, as confirmed in a multitude of studies, and shared by the American Academy of Child and Adolescent Psychiatry. Some media companies have tried to disprove this relationship, but these scientific studies show a strong connection. After decades of warnings, we can now see the results in society and on our news. And it's not just the obvious violence in some video games and films that is so harmful, but the malicious way even the supposedly nice characters regularly treat each other on kid's shows—and then make up at the end, as if no harm was done.

Look for films with healthy principles and healthy gender roles and relationships. Children learn what they live. Parents and grandparents who are proactive in vetting what their little ones and teens watch are encouraged to call other parents and grandparents onboard, so peer pressure is lessened. Look out for what is being glorified and normalized in these films. Look for films that build a strong, healthy foundation for our children.

Storytelling, especially storytelling by the wise elders, has been used for 1,000s of years to impart life wisdom and enhance our time here on earth. The role of a filmmaker/storyteller is an extremely important one. Stories reflect life and teach us about life. Therefore, conscious media can cover all topics, all genres and can be rated from G to NC-17.

What matters is what is being gloried, openly or subliminally—what is being promoted and what is being demoted.

There are what I call "almost conscious" films, that share much consciousness-raising material, but then lack the deeper wisdom that would have prevented the addition of some destructive element(s). This is why filmmakers need to do their inner work. There is no shortcut. For example, imagine a film on higher consciousness, enlightenment, and our oneness, only, it is saturated in patriarchy, featuring almost entirely male prophets, sages, mystics, teachers, and leaders, leaving out the female prophets, sages, mystics, teachers, and leaders, thus continuing the imbalance, despite the beautiful messages the film contains. There are all sorts of films that are made with good intentions but are a mixed bag of goods like this.

Though there are some conscious filmmakers, they are grossly outnumbered. With the power of the media, we need to counter the damaging material we are exposed to and put our wisest people in the crucial role of the film's director to help lead society through these difficult times. We need more wise elders, especially the mothers and wise elder women, who have learned from life and whose voices have been kept from us! With this, the Divine Feminine's nurturing wisdom can be released into our consciousness once again.

The more diversity in age, gender, race, and spiritualities of our storytellers the better, for a fuller understanding of humanity and the world. The key is that they must be wise. When done right, film has the power to raise mass consciousness, helping us to heal our planet and usher in the next step in humanity's evolution!

Effects of Removing Our Divine Mother on Politics and Leadership, War and Peace

We left an aristocratic system behind with our dreams of building the United States on a democracy. That is what our forebears envisioned for this country. But now, with our corporations and so much concentrated power at the top, we have in many ways, reverted to the unfair economic and political dynamics of that former system. We no longer have a true democracy. This is important to recognize. It will take a complete paradigm shift to get us back on track for a genuine democratic society. We need a government that works for the people, not for the top few.

For this to happen, the polarization and division in our country need to end, so we can work together to bring about needed changes. For any chance of survival as a humanity, all divisiveness between the people needs to stop. No good can come from hair-trigger reactions, where we cancel each other out for even the slightest disagreement of view, closing the door to any possibility of a healthy dialogue. With this, we invite in ignorance. The false sense of empowerment we get by bullying someone else doesn't bring anything positive to any of our lives, and it is a waste of precious time.

This imbalance and separation is an extension of the imbalance created so long ago. The media is helping to fan the flames to a dangerous degree. The "them against us" attitude won't do anymore for us. We have been set up, and we have been made weaker. There is a saying, "divide and conquer." We have been played. All of our in-fighting is keeping us too busy to see what is going on around us polit- ically, economically, environmentally, and spiritually. We are heading for global disaster if we don't work together to get ourselves and our planet onto a healing course. No more polarization. We are not falling for it! We are smarter than that! What we need now is collaboration! Working together will bring both physical and spiritual healing.

When we witness the atrocities of war and what people are capable of doing to each other, it is difficult to see humanity as fully civilized. How can people do this to other people? The insanity of war is simply shocking! How can this still be going on? We have evolved past this.

I interviewed three-time Nobel Peace Prize nominee Scilla Elworthy for a self-taped video that we posted on YouTube for free at the start of the pandemic, titled, *Wise Words in a Time of Change*. Elworthy, a peacemaker, exemplifies the feminine qualities of wisdom. She has developed strategies that would help bring global peace, which should be a priority for everyone on this planet. With our nuclear capabilities, our endless wars may destroy the earth before climate change does. Elworthy's TED Talks on non-violence and building a world without war bring hope! I wouldn't have written this book if there wasn't still hope!

Elworthy urges our leaders, as well as us, to learn the skill of conscious listening. This is where our empathetic, feminine qualities are needed. She explains that one of the most important things for building peace and prosperity is that we need to be able to place ourselves in someone else's shoes. This has been a theme throughout this book. We need to be willing to see the situation from one another's perspective. What might they be thinking or feeling? What are their fears, hopes, and wishes? If we come only from our vantage point, we won't see things as they are. We need to understand what the other person is needing and feeling to come up with real solutions.

This kind of listening to find a mutually beneficial and satisfactory answer for both sides is the opposite of what is going on in the world right now on so many urgent matters, such as the lack of consciousness around dealing with our unrestrained gun violence, instead of looking for sensible solutions that both keep people safe, while maintaining rights.

World hunger is not an issue apart from us just because we live safely in a community with an abundant food supply. We need to know what is going on in the world and what part the U.S. is playing in it. When we look into the eyes of those suffering, we are looking at ourselves, looking back at us. What one person is going through affects all of the planet. Only with conscious listening on both sides can we honor each other and get past the ignorance, the impasses and man-made divisions we are currently experiencing. It's not the typical kind of listening that we are often used to—listening to formulate our comeback or argument. That is not listening to understand. If all parties listen with the intent to better understand the other, wisdom would be gained, our problems could be solved, and hurts healed.

I am reminded of a story I read long ago that has stayed with me, though the intricate details I no longer remember. A woman was in a war-torn Middle Eastern country as one of the negotiators between her U.S. group and a terrorist group. They had knowledge that this group was planning an attack. I don't recall if it was on the U.S. Embassy or where exactly, but she was to meet with the terrorist leader or lead negotiator, in hopes of preventing the attack. She was surprised that this leader had his young son with him. Perhaps he had no one to look after the boy who was asthmatic and struggled with his breathing. This situation with the child already put this terrorist in a different light. The woman saw the concern in the father's eyes. She also happened to have a son who suffered from asthma and always carried a natural medicine in her purse, that few people were aware would help. She asked the father if she could give his son something to improve his breathing, explaining that she has a son at home who suffers from asthma. At first, the man looked confused that she would offer such a thing, but then he allowed it. He became notably grateful when he saw it worked.

The political negotiations, however, did not go well, leaving the Americans to expect the attack the next day. But the day came and went, and the attack never happened! To this day, the woman wonders if her act of kindness and the power of them both seeing the humanity in each other was what stopped it.

The Vietnamese Zen master, Thich Nhat Hanh, conveys a similar wisdom. He said that bombs, guns, and all the violence perpetrated on others do nothing to correct the incorrect perceptions that started the trouble in the first place. It's speaking and listening with love and compassion on both sides, seeing the humanity in each other, that can heal and change the trajectory. But our leaders haven't acquired this discipline or priority system. They rely on patriarchal brute force, sacrificing countless innocent lives to get what they think they want. It's ludicrous and doesn't address the core of any problem. Thich Nhat Hanh states that even the act of simply practicing the killing of people plants the seeds of anger, fear, and violence in the hearts and souls of all involved and for generations to come.

Recognizing that our chances for humanity's survival are diminishing, what do we need to change for us to once again flourish, with a bright future ahead? We need to recognize that all of life is sacred and part of the whole.

Matthew 5:43-44

> You have heard that it hath been said, Thy
> shalt love thy neighbor, and hate thy enemy.
> But I say to you, Love your enemies: Do good
> to them that hate you: and pray for them that
> persecute and calumniate you:

Do we grasp what Jesus was saying? Why have we never listened and truly taken in the meaning of his words? The war mentality that has been around for thousands of years has been disastrous. The competitive profit over the welfare of the people game plan is why we are now in trouble. We have ravished the earth—taking without thought of giving back—and Mother Nature will have the final word. There won't be a thing we can do about it. But Mother Nature is not the enemy here—we are. After the lockdowns resulted in cleaner air and a return of birds and other animals we hadn't seen in a long time, the first thing our government did when the rivers and oceans started clearing and replenishing themselves was loosen environmental protection rules for the big corporations! I sobbed upon hearing this! We must do better!

Mary Magdalene often urged the disciples to look to the good—to turn to the good! It's time that we start looking for the good in each other. Jesus never spoke of original sin! Humanity is basically good! We just need to rise to the occasion and our full potential!

In the U.S., issues have been created that shouldn't be. People shouldn't be dying in one of the world's richest countries because they don't have proper health care. Students shouldn't be in so much debt that they can't get a start in life. No one can live right if they aren't receiving a fair living wage. Women shouldn't still be needing to fight for equal rights, opportunities, and pay. Sadly, even good-intentioned politicians are stepping into a crooked system, which will go to work against them. It will take an unusually courageous leader to navigate that reality and make the needed changes.

Politics, the way we lead and govern, urgently needs to include more feminine principles. Women make up 50% of the population, yet we have never had a female president! Women are needed in the top political positions, for better representation and for the untapped perspective we bring.

Harvard psychologist Steven Pinker cites research showing that women, who possess the nurturing, mothering qualities make for peaceful and caring leaders. They tend to be a calming force and are more likely to negotiate peaceful resolutions. Carla Koppell, vice president of the Center for Applied Conflict Transformation at the United States Institute of Peace, shared that conflicts are resolved at a 35% higher rate and stay that way for 15 years if women are involved. However, according to a study in the *International Studies Quarterly,* women leaders have to contend with being called weak and are punished for looking for a peaceful resolution. Some women leaders had to become more aggressive than men to get their position and be taken seriously. Gender respect and equality are needed to allow women to govern rightly and more effectively. Cultures where women are given power are more peaceful.

Wise, compassionate women were removed from the leadership positions they held thousands of years ago, and women have been blocked from contributing what has been sorely missed ever since. We can now see what we've lost.

Today, we need women who embody the feminine principles in our top leadership positions to balance out the ideologies currently found there.

Though we are calling for leaders of any gender coming from a place of higher consciousness, what worries me is when they show up, do we even recognize them? We are so used to the soullessness of our politics, if someone came in and wisely talked about a more mindful, love-based culture, and policies where institutions put the welfare of the people and the planet over excessive profits, would we be ready to change the course of history with them, or would we find it far-fetched and mock their ideas? Would we vote in the long shot? A love-centered, fair society is what Jesus spoke of. CEOs would still make a huge profit, but in healthy, fair proportions, more like they used to decades ago.

During a sermon it was questioned if many of those who call themselves Christians today would have recognized the peace-loving Jesus, if they had they been born during his time, with their current mindset? Would they have been for or against what Jesus preached and represented? Would they have been friend or foe to him? Some honest self-reflection was encouraged, so we can heal as a humanity.

Our two-party system is a considerable part of the problem in the U.S., as it creates an extreme tug-of-war of opposites. In many other countries, more than just the top two parties have clout and a seat at the table, creating more balance in policies and decision-making. It would be beneficial to have that here.

Think about what the most important qualities are that make a great leader. Unless we have it within us to find and vote in a spiritually evolved leader, an improvement in political values and policy in the U.S. will not start at the top. It will need to start from the bottom up. We need wise people to venture into politics, so we can vote in, sane, conscious leadership on the local and regional levels, working up to the state levels and so on, to rebuild governments where the welfare of the people and our planet is a real priority, and there need to be more women included.

When finished, politics won't look like anything we have known before. Capitalism, an aristocracy, or the opposite, communism, were fatally flawed. Pretty much everything we have tried thus far has created problems. Only a massive change to a *moral* government will lead to the kind of choices that can save our earth. There needs to be a spiritual epiphany of sorts. We can pray for epiphanies for those currently in office now, but most importantly, we need to work to get the right people into office.

Speaking of epiphanies reminds me of Edgar Mitchell, the Apollo 14 astronaut who had the window seat on the way back from the moon. As they were approaching Planet Earth, his scientific mind had not prepared him for what he was about to experience. When Earth came into sight he was overcome with a feeling of interconnectivity with her, the stars, and the entire universe! He was stirred by how tiny and fragile our Mother Earth looked, recognizing that we need to give her more care. That moment changed his life forever. It moved him to establish the Noetic Science Institute, where they now study consciousness, interconnectivity, and such. To me, they are combining science with mysticism. Science and quantum physics keep proving what the spiritual masters have known for thousands of years—everything is part of the whole. Now we just need a conscious government that understands and holds this wisdom. How we govern will change meaningfully.

Effects of Removing Our Divine Mother on Business and Economics

Our economic system has been damaged by the same out-of-control patriarchal structure as our political system. Whenever one principle becomes too powerful, its lower qualities tend to take over. Without the feminine qualities to keep the masculine in balance, economics and politics have become corrupt. This goes both ways. The same could happen the other way around if the feminine became overly dominating. It's in politics and economics where the biggest global shifts need to take place for our survival. The focus on profit and growth at all costs—will be at the cost of our species.

Most of us are aware that our planet, with everyone's children and grandchildren on it, is heading for disaster. Yet, we cannot seem to find new solutions. We are trapped in the cycle, entrenched in a way of thinking and how we have always done things. We keep trying to solve our problems, while continuing all the actions that got us in trouble in the first place. We don't want to give anything up! Yet, our only hope is to radically change what we have been doing!

An imbalanced system has created the 1% wealthiest people in the world with a Grand Canyon wide wage gap between them and the rest of society. Society is in trouble because of this. A system of greed that is void of basic compassion comes from off-kilter consciousness.

This wage gap didn't exist when my parents started their lives together, and there were still plenty of very rich people. Most just didn't have more than they would ever need in a lifetime, while the people who worked for them and helped get them there didn't have enough. The old-time CEOs were likely genuinely happier. They paid their employees good, living wages. People feel better at their core when they do what's right, and equality creates a happier, healthier work environment and society. Employees work harder when they are satisfied with their pay, their lives are stable, and they can occasionally recharge with a vacation. When people feel better, they do better. The whole vibe uplifts everyone.

What makes things worse now is that the already excessively rich are the ones not paying their share of taxes that go into governmental programs meant to benefit society, such as education, health care, social security, income security, infrastructure, and so on.

Currently, many households live paycheck to paycheck and cannot survive on one paycheck alone. The middle class is struggling and isn't truly the middle class anymore. One unexpected expense or serious illness can knock a family off their feet, where their only hope to hold onto their home is to organize a GoFundMe campaign to cover medical bills. This also speaks volumes about our healthcare system. This is no longer a fair and stable society.

It seems counterintuitive to those who head corporations, but we all need to be in this for each other, for a higher quality of life on all levels, including spiritually, which most are not paying attention to. A country, a planet, is truly only as healthy and strong as all its parts.

We are told that if we don't keep growing economically, the economy will collapse. No. The opposite is true. For a healthy planet and social structure, there needs to be a realistic limit to growth—we need to reach a sweet spot. The Club of Rome's "Limit to Growth" report is still relevant today and worthy of our attention. The definition of true quality of life may be different from what we imagine. A healthier planet and a healthier, stable, fair economic structure will increase everyone's happiness score.

With scientific data to back their claims, the Earth4All report "From Equality to Sustainability" shows how more equality is needed for a sustainable planet. Without fairness and basic equality, our planet's *equilibrium* is thrown off. The planet cannot thrive, as enough people cannot contribute as fully anymore. This report describes six reasons why greater equality in our world is critical to getting through the climate crisis and other challenges. Find the link to the full report at the back of this book.

The difference between the amount of CO_2 emissions of a poor person and a rich person is colossal. A recent Oxfam report said that the total CO_2 emissions of the 1% richest people in the world is more than double the emissions of the entire poorest half of humanity! Healing the planet and humanity will require a paramount growth in consciousness in the people at the top. But it is in that state of compassionate, higher consciousness where happiness lives.

Additionally, there needs to be the recognition that insatiable economic growth must be replaced with a **focus on the well-being of society.** Wise, intelligent voices are being raised on this topic, challenging the old way of thinking, with a focus on Spiritual Economics.

We live in a capitalistic, competition-driven business culture, where growth is everything instead of the kind of quality of life that we are talking about. Our current model of greedy, non-stop growth is not sustainable on a finite planet with finite resources. Imagine if our bodies kept growing and growing. Nothing can continue to grow forever. People stop growing when they hit their prime height, and a steady economy is very similar. We are at a point where we need to find and keep it around its healthiest sweet spot.

Already in the 1800s, philosopher and political economist John Stuart Mill spoke of the eventual need for a "Steady-State Economy" where the stock of capital and the population stop growing, and instead, level off and stay calm and stable. He explained that by doing this, the art of living would continue to improve. That's right, the quality of life would go up! The time has arrived for a collaborative, fair, eco-friendly economic structure.

With patriarchy, men hold the power, and with that power comes privilege. Men working with men, creating glass ceilings difficult for women and other minorities to penetrate. When there is an imbalance in privilege, there is also an imbalance in contribution. This means, for example, that women, people of different ethnicities, and people with a different, perhaps more moral way of doing things, won't easily get in. We desperately need these diverse perspectives though for new solutions.

Corporate integrity could increase with greater equality. Currently corporations expose their lack thereof in a multitude of ways, including how their products are made. Many products now appear to be engineered to break at a certain point so they will need replacing. We have printers designed to waste ink, batteries made to eventually stop taking a charge, companies creating unconscionable amounts of waste with deceptively large containers that are filled only a quarter of the way with product—such as medications, supplements, protein powders, etc. This creates massive, unnecessary landfill waste.

It gave me hope when I heard that Yvon Chouinard, founder of Patagonia, one of the world's most popular and profitable sportswear brands, gave their company away to help save the planet. How did he do this? My understanding is that he put his company into a trust and non-profit, which is designed with the sole purpose of funneling company profits into saving our Mother Earth. Even after having done that, he was left with more than enough for himself and his family.

Not everyone will want to be this generous, but, in sharp contrast, the extreme hoarding needs to stop by those who will squeeze every last drop out of everyone else, so they can have more. Quality living is conscious living while we are here, and that means seeing our interconnectedness. Wealth can't be taken with us when we leave this world—not a dime. What is eternal is our soul, which leaves with an imprint of what we did while here—good and bad. How have our choices affected others, even people we have never met?

Changing the system starts with our individual soul work, and then a global shift in perspective, values, and priorities will follow. The time for a wiser, healthier, heart-based economic structure has arrived.

It was Buckminster Fuller who said that we can never change things by fighting the existing reality. To change something, we need to build a new model that's so good, that the old model becomes obsolete! There is cause for incredible hope in that respect! Recently, I came across three separate articles that raised awareness about a Wellbeing Economy Alliance (WEAll) that was organized a few years ago. Thus far, the governments participating in this alliance are Scotland, Iceland, New Zealand, Wales, Finland, and Canada. Reading their wisdom-filled mission statement and plans on their website can bring some much-needed optimism. They are stepping up to the plate and putting their words into action regarding many of the ideas we talked about here. They are creating an economic structure that "serves the people and the planet, not the other way around."

The Effects of Removing Our Divine Mother on Consumerism

One of our greatest threats to Mother Earth is our ravenous rate of consumption, and this is something we the people can all do something about! Much money goes into advertising to entice us with images of things we think we need but we don't, so that we will continue this insane rate of consumption. Now, like lemmings, we are heading over the cliff of climate change.

Our leaders promise to tackle global warming while tiptoeing around the fact that we need to make radical changes to our way of living to do that. If we keep consuming without limit, our planet's environmental systems, which are limited, will collapse.

Later, in the "Self-Healing" section of this book, we talk about the dramatic healing we can create for our own health through wise lifestyle changes. People who have stayed faithful to healthier lifestyles and diets have turned around conditions like diabetes, high blood pressure, and all sorts of chronic illnesses. The same could be true for the health of our planet. There absolutely are lifestyle changes we could implement that could help turn Mother Earth back around to a planet of shining health. We can't wait for others. We need to start making the changes that will help our planet ourselves. A great place to start is putting an end to our mindless rate of consumption! We, the people, have control over what we do in that arena! It's time we liberate ourselves from our shopping addiction and accumulation of too much stuff!

Shopping gives us a false sense of increased self-worth and uplifts our moods, albeit only temporarily. Mindfulness would fill that void in a much more satisfying and lasting way.

As a young woman, I sure enjoyed shopping and remember the lift it gave me. After doing my inner work, I don't need that anymore. It wasn't something I forced myself to give up, it just happened naturally. I would much rather take a walk in nature or engage in a more meaningful activity. There is no longer that void to fill. What I do now gives me true satisfaction.

What have we been teaching our kids through our words and actions? What are they being told by the media? When I observe competitive parents or grandparents, as they try to outdo the next person, proclaiming how they love to spoil their kids with things, I wonder if they realize what the word spoil means. It means to ruin or destroy. Conditioning a child to expect more and more stuff as signs of their worth is not good for that child's psyche.

It would be more beneficial to a child to show them love and affection and to teach them values that will genuinely raise their self-esteem, character, and potential for happiness—while simultaneously teaching them the values that will help with the healing of the planet. It is their future that is at stake. We can teach our children that having material goals is good, but not to overvalue things. Teach them instead to value their relationship with themselves, nature, and others. Help our children learn self-regulation and gratitude for what they have. We can teach them about the sacredness of life and God.

I am an artist, so I do enjoy a warm and aesthetic home. I especially love having a beautiful garden. This type of beauty is good for the soul. Harmonious beauty is soothing and nurturing. I look for quality items such as furniture that lasts for a long time. There is no need to be constantly buying and replacing. There are better things to do with our time and money.

We live in such an unconscious, throw-away culture. It's devastating how much people buy and then throw away. This creates damage on so many levels that we may not think about. First, we strip our earth of natural resources to make billions of products and create toxic pollution while making them. Then we throw these items away, creating mountains of landfill, so we can buy more. Consumerism is destroying the planet. It is also keeping us from doing the inner work that would bring us lasting happiness.

If we reflect for a moment, we must admit to ourselves that we don't really need all the things we keep buying. As stated above, it is best to buy something that lasts and won't need replacing for a long time. When there is a need, or one has grown tired of something, consider trading, donating, or buying gently used items. There are buy nothing groups all over where people simply give things to each other. All this is wonderful for the budget and the planet. Thrifting has become popular for a reason. I also have a friend who is great at repurposing. It is inspirational how imaginative she gets with the beautiful, useful items she creates. We can have fun with this.

Let's support companies who have integrity when producing their products and who minimize their carbon footprint in all aspects of production. Let's be selective about who we give our hard-earned money to. We have influence in this manner.

Though we may buy items online, we must make it our goal to try and cut back and buy locally when possible. Items shipped from a distance create so much more additional harm to the planet. The packaging materials that are required to wrap the individual orders become trash instantly. So much fuel is needed to fly and drive the singular items to their destinations. Now multiply this by billions of packages. That is why **a local economy is good for the planet**—made local, grown local, bought local.

Buying online also deprives us of human interaction and the pleasures of browsing. Browsing can be relaxing and uplifting. I love browsing through the local bookstore, for example, looking for my next treasure. Bookstores and libraries are my happy place. I could spend a couple of hours there. It nurtures my soul. My bookstore has a mix of used and new books. If we end up paying a couple of dollars more than if we bought the book online, that is a teeny price to pay for entertainment. It is a small price for the pleasure of being able to browse, thumb through the book, and interact with wonderful people. Occasionally the book we want can even end up being cheaper at the store, especially if we find it in the bargain section, so it evens out. If we don't support these stores, they will disappear for good!

The same goes for toy stores. If we don't support these wonderful, small local stores, they will disappear, become extinct, and the warm enjoyment and magic we gained from them will be no more. If that happens, we will become more and more isolated. These stores are part of our sense of community. To lose this would be heartbreaking, a real loss.

Let's cut way back on consumerism by trading, buying and selling used, donating, or repurposing. When we do need to shop, buy local as much as possible. Make it a point to shop wisely and consciously.

Sayings According to the Times

When reading the Bible, we can recognize that the Ten Commandments contain eternal wisdom. Yet, some of the Biblical stories were time-sensitive, meaning they were pertaining to the times in which they were written, and times have changed. Some texts were simply addressing the present situation and weren't meant to remain the same for all perpetuity. They are not applicable now under entirely different circumstances.

An example of a saying where the conditions have changed dramatically is when at the beginning of time humans (as well as birds, fish, and animals) were told to "be fruitful and multiply." This was for our survival when there were extremely few people walking the earth. This is no longer the case. In fact, the earth is becoming overpopulated, and global warming is upon us. It doesn't matter that when you look out the window, you still see plenty of space.

Can you imagine how very few people there were 3,000 years ago if in 1800 the population was under 1 billion? 1800 was only about 225 years ago. In 1900, there were less than 2 billion people. In 2000, the world population was already starting to bust at around the 6 billion mark! Now the population is projected to reach around 10 billion by 2050! That is an increase of 4 billion in just 50 years! Our finite planet can't support this accelerated increase of people and the impact this has on our ecosystem!

I was recently exploring a website recommended to me, ClubofRome.org. It saddened me how long ago this group of concerned intellectuals had been sounding the warning bells that there needed to be a limit to growth—population growth, economic growth, corporate growth, etc.—or we would end up sitting at the peak of a tipping point for the planet. This group gathered officially for the first time in 1970 in Rome, and 2 years later, their *Limits to Growth* book was published. Yet, about 50 years later, here we are sitting on the tipping point. We can point our fingers at what those in charge are doing, and indeed much of it is on them, but many of the problems fall on society's, we the people's, shoulders too! Did we just not want to believe it?

There's much for us to do on many levels. We know that we can't fill a 6 oz glass with 9 oz of water, and we must realize then that we can't keep growing on a finite planet. No one paid attention to the warnings the reports contained back when making the changes would have been easier and would have made a big difference. This is our last chance to listen. We are in a world that is starting to show the signs of shutting down.

Because of this, many people have decided to limit their family size to between zero to 3 children. Some couples may still long for a larger family though. With the inner knowing that we are all one, either right from the onset or perhaps after having a couple of biological children, is adopting a possibility? Recognizing our connection and that there are babies and children out there, alone, deeply yearning to be loved, could our hearts open to birth one or more children into our family in this way? It is a spiritual birth into the family, and that child would be ours as much as if we gave physical birth.

This would require soul-searching, because it should only be considered if one can truly love the child as much as a biological child. Otherwise, I've heard heartbreaking stories, where parents can do more harm than good when they can't.

Recently I heard talk about population collapse, which is unrealistic, given the facts. We have more people on this limited earth than we have ever had in history. We are not anywhere near such a thing as a population collapse. If we go back in time, we know there were far fewer people than there are now, with no danger of population collapse. Corporations may dislike the idea of keeping a steadier population count simply because they want more people to sell to.

Though the population is currently still rising, it is slowing down. More people are aware now that it has become urgent to put a cap on it. It's not just about eventually running out of space; it is about already running out of resources and the stress that has already been put on our complex ecosystem. We are only beginning to taste the consequences. People in the poorest countries will suffer the consequences most harshly at first, but no one will be able to escape it.

We can build these resources back up over time, if we start now. With fewer births there will be less impact on our environment; with fewer things needed, there will be less garbage and pollution to throw nature off-balance, giving it a better chance to restore itself. This is not about controlling birth rates for the sake of control. It is about doing what is needed to save this planet and all of the people we care about on it. It will take wise, radical, voluntary, positive, changes for this to happen. It will take a more conscious way of living.

Taking Care of Our Planet

Taking care of our planet by incorporating more of the feminine principle into its care means loving and nurturing all of nature and all of life because we see it as sacred. Opening our awareness to the reality that even our smallest choices impact the planet will inspire better actions. We cannot make excuses anymore about being too busy to do the right things. What we do at home matters more than we realize, from recycling to composting, to reducing product consumption by buying some things used or simply shopping less, to what we spray around our house or garden. Here are a few thoughts on some of what we can do.

Do our inner work: Heal ourselves, heal the planet!

Repair: Before throwing an item away and even before placing it in the recycling bin, we need to ask ourselves if this item can be repaired. Why throw something away and take it out of circulation, if it can easily be repaired? We can save money by repairing items that still have life in them, rather the spending the money on something new. Even if we no longer want the item, repair it and then sell it, trade it, or give it away. Keep it out of the landfill and in use.

Repurpose: This is a fun one because we get to get creative! Almost anything can be repurposed. Repurpose those empty containers. Whenever a food item comes in a glass jar, it never goes in the recycling bin at my place. It becomes a clean, reusable storage container for leftovers (no BHT) or a vase or a drinking glass. Repurposing can inspire our imagination. I've seen an old dresser turned into a bathroom vanity with a sink inserted. You can even create art out of repurposed items.

Donate, sell, and trade: We have come to a place where we realize it is not wise or responsible to throw away what is still in good shape and what someone else could use. Donate, sell, or swap regularly. It lessens what gets thrown in landfills and it can save us quite a bit of money to spend on more important things, like making memories.

Buy used: When there is something we need, we can go on a treasure hunt for that gently used gem of an item. Thrifting is economical, it is environmentally friendly, and it can be a fun thing to do, alone or in a group.

Compost: Composting is easy, and most waste disposal companies provide containers, or you can create your own by repurposing something you already have. Find out what is considered compost in your state—such as food waste and yard waste, soiled paper and napkins, etc., and adhere to the rules, because it can cause trouble on the backend if we don't. If we ignore the rules and put our compost into plastic bags, they will usually be separated from the good compost and thrown away as regular garbage. What good have we done then? We need to care enough to do it right.

Recycle: Recycle properly. Most waste companies provide a list of what can be put in each bin. Again, we don't want to put our recyclables in plastic bags, or they will most likely become trash at the recycling facility. Are we conscientiously doing our best to recycle? I'm often frustrated when I see so many recyclable items in the regular garbage and trash like greasy pizza boxes (they belong with the compost) in the recycle bin, because the grease can cause problems with the recycling equipment. Many waste companies allow us to tape used batteries to the top of the recycle bin for recycling. Recycling is the least we can do to help the planet. Recycling is a last resort for items we would be better off repairing, repurposing, selling, trading and donating. Our landfill trash bins should be nearly empty.

Dispose of toxic items properly: Properly dispose of items, such as medications we haven't used up. There are safe medicine disposal sites everywhere, which can be looked up online. Medicines flushed down the toilet can contaminate our lakes and streams, killing or hurting fish and other aquatic life. These medications can end up in our drinking water and wreak havoc on our own health. Where I live, there is a police station and drugstore that takes pharmaceutical waste.

Batteries can be dropped off at certain stores where we already normally shop, so we can combine it with another task. Some recycling companies allow us to put them on top of our bins. There are sites for toxic waste such as paint and there are e-waste sites for electronic equipment. It just takes a moment to look up the nearest, most convenient drop-offs and once we know where they are, it becomes routine.

Engage in authentic activism: Everyone has something they feel passionate about, such as returning our Divine Mother to the world's consciousness, world peace, human rights, equality, addressing climate change, principled economics, ethical politics, earth-friendly agriculture, real health care, animal rights, spirituality, and so on. The more people actively working to genuinely create the changes that will help humanity and this planet heal, the more reason for hope. If we don't know what we are passionate about yet, we can start by exploring the material at the back of this book. We can ask ourselves what natural gifts and talents do we bring to the table? How can we help? What stirs our soul?

I've included a partial action list just to get us started if there is a desire to make a difference. Younger and older generations will likely have the most time to dedicate to a chosen movement. Parents raising kids may have less extra time, as they are already busy with the important task of raising young people to become compassionate, loving, conscious human beings. For parents who are busy driving to and from school and then to and from soccer practice, tending to their children's needs, helping with homework and so much more, if there is time for activism, that is wonderful. Perhaps it is something you can do together as a family. If not, setting a good example for your children by how you live is a precious contribution.

Collaborate to help heal the planet: Join organizations or groups dedicated to healing the planet and humanity, or start your own group. Encourage others to get involved as well. Get out and speak out.

Help those in need: Join a humanitarian cause or organization where you can make a positive difference in vulnerable people's lives.

Advocate for corporate accountability: Demand fair living wages and hold corporations accountable for what they are doing and what they are putting into the environment. Climate change is accelerating, and our quality of life and health is deteriorating. Never have there been so many people with chronic illnesses. The time for change is now.

Consume less: Stop mindless buying and waste. It is liberating to free ourselves of that mentality, and it will help our planet recuperate.

Vote: Vote for positive policy changes and moral leaders with the welfare of humanity at heart, which probably means that we will be voting for someone who only has a long shot at winning the top positions. But it can't be the usual for us if we want to turn around the planet's fate. If enough of us are willing to take the leap, we can make it happen!

Choose conscious media: Be discerning regarding the media we and our families watch. It has a far greater influence on us than we think. Take the time to be selective. Ask ourselves, "What is being glorified here? Is this uplifting humanity or catering to its lowest denominator?" So much of television and film is aimed at the lowest denominator. If we want our own vibration to rise, we and our children can't keep absorbing junk into our psyches. Quality, conscious films, books, and so on, already exist, we just need to sift through the rubble and look for them, and we need much more of them. This type of media is both entertaining and satisfying to watch, as it is food for the soul.

Create conscious media and art: Artists, authors, and media makers of all disciplines are being called to use their gifts to raise humanity's vibration. Among many other things, this includes bringing a healthier, wiser, representation of the feminine into the world. As artists, we have incredible power! We want to actively work on raising our own consciousness so we can access wisdom in creating our work and with that, help to raise humanity's consciousness!

Organize neighborhood gatherings: Create a neighborhood group and encourage our friends to do the same, as this can become a wonderful form of inspiration and activism. Support each other to go green and work towards zero waste, by looking into things such as getting reusable cloth bags for the fruits and vegetables we get at the grocery store, instead of using single-use plastic bags, etc. Brainstorm. Perhaps find a common cause to get involved in. It is motivating to be part of a caring community.

Support Mother Nature: Plant trees and help with other restorative efforts. Not only do trees take in carbon dioxide, and release precious oxygen into our air, but trees communicate with each other. They are sentient beings. Nature increases our well-being. Bring it into our neighborhoods. Do not use poisons or pesticides that cause a chain of harm.

Protect our parks and wild spaces: Protect them with all we've got. Once gone they will be gone forever!

Demand healthier, more humane ways of farming and of producing our food: Heal our soil with crop diversity and crop rotation. Ask for pesticide-free, sustainable agriculture.

Pray and meditate: All consciousness shifts in the world start with us personally. Prayer and meditation shift consciousness, promote healing, and help us find balance, wisdom, and a higher way of living and loving. For an amplified effect, we can join or organize synchronized peace and global healing meditations. These events can be held online or in person.

Unify for peace: Do our part to help heal the division in this country and in this world. See beyond the lies we have been fed that keep us feeling separate from each other. We are a global community that needs to come together to heal the planet. See the humanity in each other. We are in this together. A purposeful, happy, and meaningful life must include recognizing our connection. This can become the age of great positive transformation for our planet when we do.

Taking Care of and Empowering Our Children

The best thing we can do for our children is to love them unconditionally, accept them and understand them, and then lead by example through a love-based, conscious, compassionate, integrous life. When we make a mistake, admit it and then do better so they know it is okay to make mistakes. Explain to our children that we are all constantly learning and evolving. Teach healthy self-love and self-respect, as well as love and respect for others. Gently guided character building is as essential, at an early age, as having fun. The misconception that spoiling children with material things equates to demonstrations of love can be debunked by looking up the synonyms for the word "spoil" in a thesaurus. We will come up with words such as "ruin". Much focus on material things can throw a child's priorities off throughout life. Instead, teach a healthy balance between the material and the spiritual to build good character and a healthy outlook on life.

There has been so much tragedy around bullying, especially at the schools. Conversations are necessary. Parents want to talk about how we treat others starting early in life, and we will want to stay aware of how we, ourselves, speak to and about people, especially people we may not like or agree with. Never let our words and actions become intolerant and demoralizing. Also let our children know that if bullying ever happens to them, we will be there for them, but they need to come to us and let us know. Make sure the faculty at their school is diligently doing their part as well, but the conversations and examples start at home.

Teach children principles like gratitude, kindness, and the ability to walk in someone else's shoes to help them learn compassion. Hone caring and equal friendships. We can teach them about their own self-worth by listening when they speak, this gives our child's thoughts and words value.

It is a wonderful thing when we take our children outdoors and encourage a love for nature. It is also wonderful for them when parents encourage a love for books. Nature is good for the mind, body, and soul, and good readers have it so much easier in life. Books open doors.

Parents now have something new to contend with that didn't exist before—from the time that they are born, children are bombarded by a busy, noisy, information-saturated world. With the Divine Mother returning, a more nurturing world can follow.

We'll want to protect our little children from the violence and far too adult information they can be exposed to before they can properly process it. It's vital to let children just be children for a while. Kids are not adults. They are still developing their selfhood, and they need to feel safe. It's essential for their mental, emotional, and spiritual health and for developing a solid foundation on which to build their lives. Allow them their innocence. They have their whole lives to be adults and all that comes with it. Don't force them to grow up too soon by subjecting them to information they are too young to comprehend.

Be conscientious of what our young ones are watching. How are the characters treating each other? What is being promoted? Recognize the importance of curbing time spent watching TV or on electronics, to allow valuable time for creative play and nature. The destressing nightly news can wait until they are older. Please read the section in this book on social media.

Be assured that fantasy is not a silly waste of time without benefit. Fantasy, which requires the use of the imagination, is healthy for children, as it helps them develop creative problem-solving skills for later in life. It also encourages optimism. It is good to choose toys that inspire creative play and stimulate the imagination, avoiding things such as dolls that are heavily made up or inappropriately sexualized.

Make sure children and teens have enough quiet time for reflection and rest. The pacing of life and all the activities kids are involved in these days, can become too fast and intense to be healthy. We all need time to regroup and rest.

Though women are still primarily responsible for raising the children, it is nice that many fathers are participating in parenting more than before. It is wonderful too that there is more conscious parenting going on for more people.

Parenting is one of our most important blessings and undertakings in our lives. This book talks about the significant damage to all of us that was caused by the erasure of our Divine Mother. Our deep bond with our earthly mother starts in the womb. Our most significant relationship growing up tends to be with our mother, though both parents are significant. Unfortunately, many families don't stay together these days. In a dysfunctional household or after a divorce, children's lifelong self-worth and emotional well-being can be inadvertently damaged by the toxicity created by feuding parents.

In the case of divorced parents, a toxic response would be where the noncustodial parent senses that the custodial parent will have a closer relationship with their child or children. The primary parent tends to be the mother, but not always. The noncustodial parent then sets out to undermine this vitally important relationship. For example, they may

do this by verbally abusing the mother in front of the child/
children whenever they come around, hoping to damage the
loving bond and this parent's authority, as well as the child's
perception of them, in an attempt to make themselves look
better. It doesn't take much to realize that doing this would
pull the rug out from under their developing child, damaging the very foundation they are building their lifelong
emotional and mental stability on. It can also affect their
ability to have healthy relationships. The target may be the
other parent, but the biggest victims when something like
this goes on are always the child/children.

Divorces are rough on the heart and ego. Yet, I don't
know too many parents who would conscionably want to
harm their child in this way if they gave their actions more
thought. Parenthood requires selfless love. It means taking a
deep breath and taking our ego out of the mix. The moment
we realize we have made a mistake of great consequence, we
will want to find the courage to acknowledge it within ourselves and stop the destructive behavior in its tracks. From
that moment on, make the choice to do better. When we
review our lives, we want to know that we did right by those
we love. Support the parent instead, and remember to treat
each other with respect, especially in front of the children.
We are either acting out of love or out of fear. Choose love.

Lead by example. Teach our children peace, love, and
respect. Let them know that we love them unconditionally;
that they are precious; that life is precious; that we are all
connected, and that we are all part of God.

It is wise to have conversations with our children early
on about God and our oneness. Nothing will enhance their
awareness and their quality of life more than knowing God's
love. Let them know their life has a purpose. The times are

uncertain. I believe that the good in us will prevail and that humanity's consciousness will rise, so we can heal our planet. If that doesn't happen, what could take place in the future for the youngest generation, or the one following, is unbearable to think about.

Let's do all we can so that the evolution to a higher way of being here on Earth is what happens. To do that, we must become aware of how we are living. What can we, as parents and grandparents, do to help ensure our children have a future? For parents, this depends on how much time we have left over after the primary responsibility of parent-ing.

Seniors who feel they have worked hard their entire lives and are now ready to retire, travel, or just enjoy taking it easy—wonderful. Enjoy your well-earned retirement and God bless. For those seniors and grandparents who feel differently and want some of what retirement holds, but mourn not being more active, there is a mighty call to action! Your life still has an immense purpose, and we need what you have to contribute. Leave a legacy. Get behind a cause you are passionate about or create your own, and make a difference! If we multiply this type of action by the masses of grandparents on this Earth, we have a powerful force for good!

Social Media

With the true connector of all life taken from our consciousness, poor replacements appear. Social media is another culprit throwing society off balance. Social media does have its pros as well as its cons. It can connect us with people across the world and with friends we normally would never see. It connects us with other cultures. It provides entertainment and a platform for self-expression. It's wonderful for promoting what we are selling. But there is no denying the multiple unhealthy aspects to it.

Social media is primarily a superficial connection where people tend to put up phony fronts. Everyone's life looks great on the internet. This seems to lead to more depression and anxiety in society, when we compare our real lives to what we see on other's posts. Social media is a big culprit in spreading false news. People of all ages can hide behind this platform to cyber bully and exact harm on others, with sometimes devastating results.

We don't appreciate the natural unfiltered beauty of nature all around us, or even our own natural, unfiltered beauty anymore. Primarily women are under this pressure. Social media has created a fake, filtered world, with a disturbing impact on our self-image and mental health. There is a danger in getting caught-up in this self-presentation mode. According to four studies cited in "Psychology of Women Quarterly", it can trigger the psychological issue of self-objectification and self-sexualization.

Social media can create couch potatoes and keep us from getting out and really living! It can also give us a false sense of activism. We post a political article or something on climate change and feel like we've done something. Well, we haven't—not really! We need to get out and get involved in a cause or movement that we care about. That's real-life activism, with real impact.

In 2021, former Facebook executive Frances Haugen leaked thousands of documents to expose that the potential harm of these platforms was known by those building them. Now there is another new lawsuit presented by devastated parents who say that their children or teens have been put in danger or have died, due to social media. They cite a dramatic sudden rise in depression and suicide among teenagers, in the U. S., especially in teenaged girls. They say this increase happened at the same time as an upsurge in social media use about a decade ago, with new apps being introduced that drew in young users. Parents argue that much more can be done to keep the children and teenagers safe on these platforms, but they claim that profit is being chosen over safety. They point out that part of the problem is the algorithms that take the young to unhealthy content, such as images and stories of anorexia after innocently looking up "dieting." They can, at the time of the writing of the article, be led to dangerous content including instructions on how to self-harm. The parental controls features are easy to navigate around, and the age checker is basically useless. These parents are passionate about changing this and getting real protections in place for our children.

Even if more protection becomes mandatory, nothing can protect children completely. It is wise to educate ourselves on what they are being exposed to through these platforms. The suggested articles in the back of this book are a good place to start.

Social media is addicting. We all know that. Over time, it can literally steal years from our lives. Imagine what we could accomplish if we had the hours back. There's a fabulous documentary, titled, *The Social Dilemma,* which I highly recommend watching to make us aware and help us take our power back, at least in the time department.

AI will take away a colossal amount of our jobs. It's already starting to happen, and it can get to the point where it creates a disaster for humanity. Corporations go with what saves them money. Before that happens, according to the *Forbes* article, "AI Bias Could Put Women's Lives at Risk", there is already a current threat posed to women and minorities with the biases engrained in AI, through the men who are creating it. Apps can give dangerous misguided health advice to women, as one example, because men are inputting the data with a limited understanding of the female body and can rely on misinformation online about women's health—and the list goes on. I became deeply concerned when I read the several articles at the back of this book.

Besides the danger of biases, I read about the looming threat that AI can get out of its creators' control. According to the *Associated Press* article, "4 Dangers That Most Worry AI Pioneer Geoffrey Hinton," AI is about to become more intelligent than us, and Hinton, the godfather of AI, doesn't know how humanity will survive that! I wrote this book because I believe good will prevail and that there is hope that we can transform and raise humanity to its higher vibration to save our planet. Though there are some positives when I read about what the concerning things happening with AI, I felt some of that hope evaporate, and I wondered, "Is this what the Bible warned us about?" I recommend reading the article. We need to stay active and alert regarding where AI is heading, while also taking the time to pray for the best.

The Mental Health Crisis

As would be expected with such an imbalance and so many issues present in the world, mental health is more likely to be thrown off balance as well. Especially with signs of climate change upon us, along with the COVID-19 epidemic and the isolation that followed, many of us feel hopeless about the future. What is extra concerning is the drastic increase in mental health issues in children, teens, and college students. They need extra family support.

Forbes cites a study spearheaded by Dr. Sarah Lipson at Boston University that found that the mental health of college students has been going down steadily for about a decade now, with a startling overall 135 % rise in depression and a 110 % increase in anxiety. Everyone has their ups and downs regarding how they feel mentally. No one feels perfect all the time, but what they are talking about here is a serious drop in mental and emotional well-being. I touch upon some of what could be contributing to this in other parts of the book, including the children's and social media sections.

Many changes in the world are harming young people's outlook on life and their future—global warming, endless wars, school safety, an unfair economic system, social media, artificial intelligence tools with their possible privacy risks and ability to replace jobs, student debt, and so much more.

On top of the dark prognosis given for the planet's future, the stress level created by needing to find our way through a labyrinth of wrong turns and misdirected, automated AI help is detrimental to all of us—the reduction in daily human contact is even worse. We just need to look at our homeless population to see that the world is in a mental health crisis and that our current system is failing us. There are people in jail who wouldn't be there if they got the mental health support they needed when they needed it and for the length of time they needed it.

In the current construct, with our government's current priorities and how the health care system is set up, not nearly enough is being done to help what is going on in this arena in a way that is effective and long-term. There are wait lists for therapists for people who urgently need support for their or other's safety. Mental health care is expensive and proper care often requires a year or two of commitment and may need to take place in a care facility. Yet, these specific therapies that would benefit an individual the most are often not covered by insurance. There needs to be a government-covered program to support mental health.

I believe many conditions can be healed with the right support system and methods, along with persistence. Mental health issues need to be destigmatized and given the same care as physical health issues.

It is said that mindfulness in combination with such modalities as dialectical behavior therapy (DBT) and cognitive behavioral therapy (CBT), can heal or significantly improve quite a few mental health issues and disorders, not to mention improve quality of life in general.

They have also seen results with a combination of mindfulness practices, better nutrition, and proper sleep. Many of us don't realize that the types of foods we eat affect our gut health, which can have a surprising effect on our brain and mental health. A link has been found between an imbalance of bacteria in the microbiome and depression and other mental health issues. Sugar and our highly processed foods can create a serious imbalance. So, getting the proper nutrients is vital for mental balance, as well as avoiding the highly processed foods that harm our gut.

Sleep deprivation can dangerously change a person's brain chemistry, making them behave in ways and make decisions they normally wouldn't. Getting enough quality sleep nightly is critical for our emotional and mental health.

Our attitude affects our quality of life, but it gets taken too far these days. In a world where positive thinking is often pushed as a cure-all, we need to know that it is okay to feel vulnerable, overwhelmed, and sad sometimes. We can do all the right things and still have times when we don't feel good. Know that you are not alone and be easy on yourself.

There is a wonderful short video titled, *Don't Tell Me to Just Breath*, that shares how meditation, and those types of things alone are not always enough to change the feelings of depression and anxiety, because what caused the depression and anxiety is still there. What helps is to also take constructive action and get out there and do something about the issues in the world! Sometimes taking the focus off of ourselves for a moment and volunteering or getting behind a cause can bring us a sense of purpose in life, which can be extremely healing and empowering, especially when combined with mindfulness and self-care. The feeling of loss of control will be diminished, which can improve our outlook. Make a difference. We get more back than we can imagine, and the feeling of being part of a community is lovely as well!

Let's insist on a healthcare system that supports our mental and physical health, and let's get out there to heal what ails society and causes such a loss of equilibrium in the first place.

Self-Healing with the Help of Nature

Most of us have warm memories of our mothers sitting bedside, caring for us when we were sick as children, pouring their hearts and souls into doing all they could to help us heal. Our Divine Mother tends to our wounds, and she has designed nature to help nurture and care for her children. I am not a medical professional, so nothing in this book is meant to be medical or any other type of advice. Consult your physician before trying something new. I am simply sharing my reflections, findings, and experiences.

It seems that our healthy link to nature has been severed. With our food manufacturing system void of much of its mothering energy, we are being fed so many heavily processed foods that we are no longer receiving proper nourishment for our bodies, which has affected our physical and mental health. Many of the foods we consume are so removed from nature that they are low in nutrients and high in harmful ingredients, which has created serious health issues in society.

I remember telling a friend that the popular brand of bread she was buying was not real bread. I joked that it was as nutritious as eating a napkin. She called me many months later letting me know that my comment had caused her to shove the bread to the back of her fridge that day, and then she forgot about it. Months later, she decided to do a deep cleansing of her fridge and found that loaf of "bread" again, still looking exactly as it did when she purchased it! It hadn't changed or decayed even a bit! Real food decays, wilts, and gets moldy because, well, it's food! Seeing it in such an excellent, plasticky condition concerned her enough to start making more conscious choices regarding what she puts in her body.

There are companies that will use better, healthier ingredients for the same product when sold in Europe versus when sold in the U.S., since our government here has allowed corporations to use the cheaper, harmful ingredients in the foods we eat and give to our children. This is beyond disturbing. People are speaking up. In California, they finally banned some of these dangerous ingredients, requiring the manufacturers to replace them with the healthier options they already use elsewhere. I hope this ban grows statewide.

We need safer practices in growing and manufacturing our foods. There have been too many food safety recalls lately. It is time to put the welfare of people over profit and grow and manufacture our foods more wisely, using higher standards.

When trying to stay healthy, I never underestimate the healing benefits of food and lifestyle changes. It takes commitment though. Eating consciously would be a significant lifestyle change for many people. We fall for advertising and are now addicted to what are, on many levels, fake nonfoods. They keep us unhealthy and grabbing for those pills. Processed foods and the toxins they contain can raise our blood pressure, our cholesterol, our blood sugar, disrupt our endocrine system, and create memory issues, behavioral issues, life-threatening illnesses, damage our gut (which affects everything), and so much more.

The clever language used in advertising these foods can mislead us into thinking they were made with our health in mind. A life-supporting, healthy diet consists of real, live foods, as nature presents them, instead of the high sugar, artificial ingredient, genetically modified, sprayed, and pro-cessed foods we are being inundated with.

As we become more conscious, eating meat comes into question, and it is unconscionable how farm animals are often treated while alive. I often reflect on the cycle of life that is all around us. We are eating a living being. I always have a difficult time watching those cycle of life segments in nature documentaries. As humans, do we believe that meat is a necessary complete protein for our health, or is it pos-sible to combine incomplete proteins, beans with rice, for example, to create the complete protein from other sources?

We know that Americans seem to eat far too much meat to be healthy. We have gone off the deep end, compromising our own health and the health of the planet along the way. Many people eat more than a serving of meat a day, a lot of it being fatty meat, and then wonder why they experience sluggishness, high cholesterol, heart issues, or other health problems. Medical professionals suggest that we would be healthier if we didn't eat so much meat and replaced some of it with servings of nuts, beans, seeds, lentils, tofu, ama-ranth, spelt, and quinoa. Luckily, I love the taste of those things. If meat continues to be part of our diet, keeping it at the maximum of one serving of meat per day, 4-5 days a week, (yes, the sausage on our pizza counts), aiming for at least 2 meatless days a week, seems to be more ideal—for our own health and for the health of the planet.

I enter the processed food sections of the grocery store for only a few select items. I mostly shop on the parameters where the real food is. Eating an organic, well-balanced diet, with plenty of vegetables and fruits, whole grains, dairy (if you aren't sensitive to them), healthy fats (olive oil, etc.), and proteins, is ideal. Try making vegetables a significant ingredient and part of our diet. Consuming nearly no added sugars or processed foods, and getting enough exercise, water, sunlight, and sleep are all important. It's so basic, yet many of us have gotten our health derailed by the commercial, non-foods filling our stores. As we become more conscious, we will naturally start gravitating toward the things that nurture and help us care for ourselves better.

I remember, years ago, getting ready to purchase a semi-precious gemstone necklace in a boutique, that came with a printed card explaining that the stone had stress-relieving properties. The woman standing near me said, "That's so beautiful I wish I could buy one, but I am Christian, and using stones for healing is witchcraft." Christians wear precious gemstones such as diamonds and rubies all the time. They are no different. All stones have subtle energy. Understanding the energies can be useful. Working lovingly with Mother Nature is our birthright. However, for stones to have that subtle effect, I was told they would need to be good-sized, not the typical size of stones in our jewelry. Still, it's wonderful to know about them and their healing properties.

So much of our personal power and control was taken from us when our own healing powers and the healing powers of nature were made taboo. The history of gifted healers being burnt at the stake as witches is a topic unto itself. Most were simply using God-given gifts found in nature to help the people of their community heal. It is sad that this woman I met at the store worried that working with the gifts of nature lovingly and with good intentions is a negative thing.

The highly respected, medieval Benedictine abbess, or Mother Superior, we talked about earlier, Hildegard of

Bingen, was such a healer. She was often called upon for advice, even by her male superiors due to her gift of intuitively recognizing specific healing properties in nature. She was a master herbalist who believed in the therapeutic power of plants and flowers, and she even worked with precious and semi-precious stones! She believed that plants, herbs, stones, and certain foods could help heal our mind, body, and spirit. That's the beauty of it, nature can heal more than just the physical.

Though Western medicine is lifesaving and is often the place to seek help when sick, it is hard not to notice that our culture is too dependent on medications, with their often serious side effects. We can turn to these too quickly rather than working with our bodies—first, on staying healthy and then find ways to activate our body's own capacity to heal when a health challenge comes up. These are things that don't seem to be covered enough in medical school.

In conventional Western medicine (allopathic), we are told too quickly that, "there is a pill or a surgery, for that." When surgery or taking medications is necessary, then do the surgery and take the pills. That goes without saying! As mentioned before, allopathic medicine can be a lifesaver, especially in emergency situations. With the advances in medicine, there is much to be grateful for. However, it is also good to be aware of what is talked about in the *Time* magazine article, "Big Pharma Is Hijacking the Information Doctors Need Most." The article reveals that for decades pharmaceutical companies have taken control over the majority of our clinical research. This is alarming.

I know of people who, towards the end of their life, are taking up to 9 pills every night and every morning. What I noticed is how one pill created a new side-effect and new issue, which they then needed to take another pill for. Though sometimes medications are necessary, it is good to know about some of the natural options that help us maintain our health and aid in healing. Natural methods can, at times, require persistence, work, discipline, or permanently changing our habits. Many people don't want to put in the effort. It would be beneficial to change our attitude from, "Ugh, I need to do this to be healthy"—to, "I get to do this to be healthy!"

Additionally, it appears that Western medicine has recently become more compartmentalized, where a cardiologist will primarily study the heart, instead of the whole body for interactivity, and interconnectivity. I am always surprised by how little doctors are taught about nutrition. Proper nutrition can often keep us off the meds.

Eastern medicine is more integrative. In integrative medicine, they not only recognize the interconnectivity of the physical body more, but they also acknowledge how emotions can have a direct effect on physical organ systems. For example, grief and sorrow are held in the lungs. Zhineng Qigong sound healing can help when grief is damaging the lungs. There are times when alternative medicine could be the better choice for us, or at the very least, complementary to our Western care (though we always want to confirm there aren't unsafe contradictions, especially with supplements and herbs). There are often options that strengthen and work with the body with less harmful side effects.

What Hildegard of Bingen had understood in her healing methods and what society lost touch with is that since everything is energy, healing ourselves energetically is extremely potent. Even our thoughts and actions have energy and can affect our well-being.

I have witnessed astonishing healing and improvements over time with Zhingeng Qigong, which is a form of energy healing. Bianca Molle, a schoolteacher from Northern California, healed herself of Parkinson's. After the month-long Zhineng Qigong Intensive she participated in, she had the discipline to continue to do the practice for 3 hours a day for a year. She still does it for not quite as long to this day! She had split the 3 hours into 1.5-hour sets. Not everyone has that kind of self-motivation and faith. She said that she literally felt the disease unwind itself like a corkscrew. Symptoms that she had felt earlier on but had gone away since the disease had progressed to worse symptoms, came back in reverse sequence. They then healed one by one until her symptoms were gone. She was declared Parkinson's free.

Most doctors will not give Zhineng Qigong credit for Molle's healing, even though she personally felt the reversal of her illness, as it happened. Instead, they attribute it to spontaneous healing that can occasionally happen to anyone. Doctors said the same to me when I reversed my collapsed lung through the Zhineng Qigong sound healing practice. I could incrementally feel the healing taking place with the sounds. I used the same method practiced in the medicine-less hospital in China, where qigong was the main method of healing. It was shut down by the government when they put a limit on how many people could gather in one place. Many healings of challenging illnesses had taken place at that hospital working with chi energy.

There are many alternative practices to choose from that can have health, anti-stress, and healing benefits, such as better **nutrition**—that's a big one and **acupuncture**, where the practitioner inserts very thin steel needles into the patient's skin at specific points, helping to rebalance the body's energy, or chi (qi). Then there's **integrative medicine** which uses a combination of therapies. **Prayer** and **meditation** are powerful daily practices. **Sound healing, yoga, massage, reiki, nature therapy**, and **essential oils** can all are said to have benefits and support our healing. They tend to stimulate our healing processes, usually in mind, body, and soul, rather than repressing or controlling symptoms.

Often, to heal our body there needs to be a permanent, favorable change in lifestyle, habits, and way of thinking and reacting. While working on this, there are supportive tools one can use.

Due to losing our divine connection, our emotions and psyche are often out of balance. In my experience, flower essences can help subtly with that. Flower essences aren't meant to cover up issues and they have no scent as they consist of the energetic essence of the flower only. They are designed to assist us primarily on the emotional and spiritual level. We can imagine the value of getting help in such a way. These vibrational energy remedies are said to bring about profound inner transformation over time. We still need to do our inner work, but flower essences are to significantly aid the process when used properly and for the correct length of time.

To truly be healthy, I have found that it is vital to get enough quality sleep. Sleep is critical for physical, emotional, and mental health. We are so busy, we don't get enough of it, not realizing that we get more done the next day when we do. But it is more serious than just that. Sleep deprivation can detrimentally alter our brain chemistry. An article on the Stanford Medicine website talks about its dangers. Sleep deprivation affects cognition, concentration, and our ability to cope with our emotions to, at times, a frightening degree. It is vital to make a clear decision for a better life, with a healthier body and mind, to commit to getting more quality sleep. The positive changes can be dramatic.

In the *National Geographic* article, "Fruits and Vegetables are Less Nutritious than They Used to Be," they say that there is mounting evidence that even our produce isn't as healthy as it used to be, due in part to the methods used to grow foods, even some of the mass-produced organic foods. Wise and careful supplement use can support healing and staying healthy, but we need to learn all we can first and not overdo it. A healthy, locally grown, organic diet is always the first choice. But, as mentioned, there are times a supplement may be needed. Allicin garlic, for example, can help fight serious infections. I have had much luck with it. But realize that it can also thin the blood, so we would need to stop taking it for at least 10-14 days before surgery, to avoid issues with bleeding. Other supplements can thin the blood as well—so we need to do our research!

I always try to make my choices thoughtfully and get professional guidance. A wise, integrative medical doctor once said to me, "Whatever has the power to heal you, also has the power to hurt you." Don't think because it is natural, it is benign. When used correctly, the right natural choices can heal. If used incorrectly, they can do harm, just like any medicine.

I find that since we are nature, simply getting out in nature to decompress and connect, allowing ourselves to feel the awe of it all, can do so much for our mental and physical health. It is not a small thing. And with everything being connected—when we heal ourselves, we heal the world!

Beauty Heals

There is healing power in beauty. It soothes and nurtures the soul. Beauty inspires and uplifts us. In cities where there is a high crime rate, adding plants, revamping buildings more aesthetically or adding structures of art coincides with a drop in criminality.

Beauty makes people feel better inside, bringing about hopefulness and optimism. Why then when planning architectural design or drafting a blueprint for city or town development, is there often not nearly enough effort put into aesthetics and real creativity? Why are we so often stuck with the plain, dull, and simply functional? The attractiveness and the energetic flow of the design, along with the incorporation of greenery amongst the concrete and designated green areas, needs to become the new standard. It baffles me that it is not. If we don't put in that extra creative effort to add inspirational beauty and a peaceful flow to the mix, we lose the opportunity to nurture the human soul of everyone who lives there and everyone who passes through. Adding more streetlamps, for example, makes a city safer. When adding streetlamps anyway, why not make them attractive streetlamps? Add both safety and inspirational beauty.

The feminine is associated with beauty, nature, creativity, and gracefulness. She understands its healing strength. When talking about beauty that heals, we are not talking about superficial beauty or the new trend of using artificial filters on our faces to create a faux beauty. This type of pretend, simulated beauty can lead to more depression and dissatisfaction. No, we are talking about the genuine beauty found in the uniqueness of each of our faces. We are talking about real beauty, in the curves of a gorgeous structural design or the beauty we find in awe-inspiring abundance in the natural world.

Appreciate the magnificence. Think of the beautiful diversity God purposefully created for us. If we go to Hawaii, we find palm trees and beaches and if we head to Alaska we gaze upon snow and completely different terrain, and on and on—and the same goes for the different people in God's design. The variety of people in the world is not meant to be hate inducing; it is meant to be awe inspiring!

Natural beauty is exiting. Especially in low-income neighborhoods, where this type of inspiration would be most important, no effort appears to be made, with the main excuse being that it is too expensive, hence keeping people trapped in this gray, hopeless environment. But the big expense is a false assumption. Something beautiful does not necessarily need to cost more. It can, if there is a budget for it, but it doesn't need to if the budget is small. What it does take is creative thinking and a conscious effort to create an environment with an uncongested, healthy flow—designs that have creativity and a feeling of harmony. It takes thoughtful effort.

There is proof that when neighborhoods are beautified, the crime rate goes down, as the new tranquil, harmonious beauty in place of the stressful, congested, disarray that was there before brings an energizing shift, along with the feeling of possibility and hope. And we all know the saying, "No one is more dangerous than the person without hope." Crime costs the city money. Therefore, wouldn't spending money to create an environment where that is lessened be so much more beneficial on all levels?

I included a link in the back of this book to information posted by the National Library of Medicine that states that a collection of several studies has revealed that living in green areas promotes mental and physical health, especially if these areas present opportunities for physical activity. I would venture to include that green spaces promote spiritual health as well. Especially pedestrian-friendly areas reduce stress and help us to recover from the stress we have experienced throughout the day. All nature areas, big or small, connect us to something bigger than ourselves.

Creating a nurturing environment in our own homes is essential. Refresh and protect the home exterior with the most eco-friendly paint available, and get rid of energy-sapping clutter, plant trees, and tend to the garden. Getting rid of clutter is a must for our well-being. When creating a nurturing environment for us we need to realize that it is not about constantly buying things for the home that we soon throw away and replace; that's actually stressful. Instead, it is recommended that we create quality design and buy things that last, keeping them around for a long time. We are now free to spend our money on meaningful things such as ethically grown, nutritious food, our loved ones, memory-making experiences, etc.

It was sad to drive through what could have been the most charming, little historical town. It could have been magical. But there was no tender-loving care given to any of the buildings or homes. Everything had become dilapidated. It's when we let structures go, when we don't refresh the protective paint, that they become expensive to repair. I worry about losing these gems without our appreciation and conscious care. I have gone through towns or visited friends where I know the median income is good, yet the care given to their property is lacking. They don't realize how much it would uplift their happiness level if they put some thoughtfulness and effort into their home. We waste too much of our time stuck on social media, instead of tending to our environment and our real relationships. What we surround ourselves with affects us. Surround ourselves with meaningful beauty that brings us joy.

It is a real struggle to keep one's personal space tranquil and pleasing when dealing with poverty, however. When the money is not there, it is a challenge just to make basic repairs or stay above water in general. If we are renting, and repairs are the landlord's duty, there is even less control over our environment, especially if they are not staying on top of things. This is another issue stemming from the extremely uneven distribution of wealth in this country that needs addressing. It's difficult to find motivation when our environment keeps us feeling down. So, any beautification effort one can put forth is worth it to help raise spirits.

In the documentary, *Stewart Udall: The Politics of Beauty,* Udall is called, "A champion of our national parks and scenic beauty, an advocate of the arts and sustainable urban design." Udall was ahead of his time. Decades ago, he understood our need for national parks for everyone to enjoy, regardless of economic status. He already felt an urgency back then to protect our wild spaces. Besides the vital benefits they bring to a sustainable planet, being out in these wild spaces can improve our physical, emotional, mental, and spiritual health. Yet, the wild is constantly under the threat of being permanently taken from us. May we fight with all our might to hold onto them. When overwhelmed, we can feel God's presence there. Protect it, honor it, get out, and enjoy it. Beauty heals!

Brave Young Voices Rising

Youth activism has been on the rise, forced upon them by devastating current events. The young people are shaking society out of its complacency. We have Greta Thunberg and Jamie Margolin on climate justice. These young people are fighting for their futures. We have Emma Gonzalez and David Hogg, the Parkland shooting survivors who are demanding reasonable gun laws for school safety. Then we have Malala Yousafzai, who is a Pakistani female education activist. She is the youngest person to have won the Nobel Peace Prize at 17. We have Autumn Peltier, the Indigenous water-rights activist who inspires our youngest citizens to protect the environment, and there are many others.

Because the older generation of politicians isn't taking any real action to solve humanity's problems, these activists are campaigning to get young people into office and shake wake us up. We need them and their perspective. They have experienced threats while growing up, that the older generation hasn't.

It is not that no one older cared before. There have been generations of environmentalists and activists before them sounding the alarms. The speaking up isn't new. What is different now is that we are getting so close to the tipping points that these young people are understandably even more impassioned because of what can happen in their lifetimes, and because of the urgency, more people are listening.

May this new energy revitalize those who have lost hope after fighting for the planet for decades and decades, realizing nothing significant had been done by those in power to change the trajectory of the planet in all that time. Get up to stand with the young. While there is life, there is hope.

Engaging the Wise Elders

Many of our new social and political activists come straight out of university with a fire in their hearts focused on what needs changing in society. The young activists will be heard. Youth is revered in this country. They will help break us out of our dangerous rut. However, there is a group that is underutilized in this culture and that is the wise elders (the key word being wise), especially the wise elder women, who are often overlooked. We can't do this without them. It is critical to combine youthful inspiration with the insights of the elders, whose wisdom comes from a long life well-lived, with many lessons learned. If we don't work together, in our enthusiasm, we are destined to repeat some serious mistakes, only appearing to be different.

From childhood on, with every year, our scope of understanding grows. By the time we are around eighteen to twenty years old, we start taking on adult responsibilities. Emerging science states that the brain's rational part is said not to fully mature until around age twenty-five, and some-times later for men. Most teenagers and young adults still filter information primarily through the amygdala, which is linked with emotional processes, rather than the frontal cortex that adults mainly use, which regulates reason. These age groups can see the same situation in a different light. Collaborating would be extremely fruitful.

Even after adulthood, ideally, we never stop growing and learning from life, hence the saying, "If I only knew then what I know now." No matter how wise someone is when they come into the world, and there are many wise young people, if receptive to learning from the heart they will be even wiser 10 years from now. Conversely, not all old people are wise, this goes without saying. It is the wise elders who need to be called forth, who have the advantage of wisdom and hindsight, to share their insights.

Unless it's been lived, it may be hard to fully understand the struggles that came before we got here, what women have experienced, and how hard we fought to get to where we are now. It was the same for us, when we were young, with our parents. I can try to imagine what they went through, but I didn't experience it. Women are still standing on more fragile ground than we might think. We have a long way to go, despite being in a better place than before. The "she", the feminine, was taken out of God. Women and girls have not been seen as part of God the same way men have been—all this time. My mother wasn't legally allowed to have her own bank account for part of her adult life, without a man co-signing, and can we count how many women presidents we have had?

When making changes in society, it is wise for all groups to sit at a round table with their unique lenses of perception—truly listen as well as talk—and work together for solutions that benefit everyone. There is a need for a balanced fuller view. The new generation will bring great drive and ingenuity. The wise elders bring hindsight with life experience. Together they will bring conscious foresight and positive change.

With our loving Mother's return, the previously invisible mothers and grandmothers will finally be able to contribute their much-needed feminine wisdom, alongside the wise elder men. With all genders, races, religions, and ages participating, we all stand a chance.

Balance

I was talking to a neighbor about the need for the feminine to be brought back in balance with the masculine for a healthy planet. Her response was, "Forget about bringing it in balance, women need to take over—men have messed this place up!" My response to this is, no, no, that is not what we want! It may be that we went from a matriarchy to a patriarchy, and neither was right for both genders. We don't want to knock the see-saw in the other direction and once again bring imbalance upon our earth. The planet can't take any more of that. We need to get off the see-saw. All genders have much to bring to the table. We are at a do or die turning point with this planet—the proof is all around us. We can't tip the scales out of equilibrium with payback for the discriminations of the past. There is no time for that and why would we want to? It's destructive! We need to stop tripping each other up and instead imagine a thriving, harmonious world where there is equality and we live with mutual respect, mutual care, mutual contribution, and in partnership.

Speaking up for our rights and taking just action against injustices is crucial—retaliation is a completely different thing. Using an extreme example, the film *Mystic River* (spoiler alert) is a haunting anti-retaliation film. No matter how justified it felt at the time, both men who exacted revenge destroyed their mental health and then their lives. Whether it's what was done to us, or what we went through due to gender, race, religion, or sexual orientation, the more spiritually whole we become, the more we realize that we cannot find happiness in that toxic state. Imbalance can only be healed with balance. Equality fosters balance.

God Energy

My circle of friends and acquaintances have a broad range of beliefs, ranging from Christianity to Buddhism, Judaism to shamanism or antagonism to atheism, etc. I care for them all. In general, they are wonderful people with strong ethics, regardless of their varying philosophies and views. If we were to talk about spirituality, there would be some serious debates. Most of my friends have a knowing, a sense that there is more to our existence than meets the eye. We can talk for hours about it. We try to find our way through the many manmade rules and regulations, to find the core teachings, which have many common threads.

A couple of friends have been so turned off by the fear-baseness of some religions, that it has turned them off to God. Depending on our upbringing around the topic of God, fear can unfortunately be preached. One of my friends expressed his fear of being constantly judged and the anxiety that brings him. My other friend is more of an antagonist and just does not feel the connection or any kind of certainty about whether or not there is a God.

My acquaintance the atheist maintains that anyone who believes in God does so out of fear. That's a very broad presumption and statement. I suppose some do—and I suppose it goes both ways. Some will latch onto God out of fear, and some will turn away from God out of fear. I can vouch that being motivated by fear is far from the truth for myself and a great many people on this planet. I do have the highest possible reverence for God, and that brings all sorts of emotions with it, but the predominant emotion is love. Being part of God is something that is sensed and understood on a soul level. I felt it as a child already, especially when

I played outside in nature or gardened, or in the evening when I looked up at the stars, and when the world was quiet, and I lay in bed to pray; I simply felt magic. I felt God.

Though we spoke about and worshiped God, I did not grow up in a strict religious household. We went to church, but not every Sunday. Still, I felt God's presence in my life. Trusting in God doesn't give us all the answers, rather it does put us on a journey. Those who have had spiritual experiences can attest that it takes great courage to open to God and the spirit world and not close up in fear! People who have had these types of events share that it can take many years to let it sink in, to gather courage, and to move forward with the journey. Whether we believe, or not believe—each lifetime we are finishing up lessons and learning new ones. What we don't learn, we are likely destined to repeat. That is the evolution of the soul.

There are those who see God as a universal energy, recognizing its intelligence. Einstein said everything is energy. With what I have experienced, along with what I have gained through my studies—I understand that to mean everything is God. It doesn't matter what name we give to God or God's energy; we are still talking about God. In Qigong, we talk about an interconnecting web of life that permeates all, and we call it chi (or qi). When we talk about the Holy Spirit, we also describe her as the Interconnecting Web of Life. Others refer to the energy that permeates all of life as Gaia, a feminine energy that is recognized as having intelligence. It is said that Gaia birthed the Cosmos and keeps every minute detail of life and existence in order. We can see the common threads among all these beliefs.

Religion and science often coexist. In an old 2009 Pew Study, it was revealed that 51% of scientists have faith in

God or a higher universal intelligence! Though that is much less than the general population, it is still a great number of scientists who are believers.

Allan Sandage is considered one of the most prolific astronomers of our time. His accomplishments include the discovery of quasars and radio-quiet quasars, measuring the expansion of our universe, and the list goes on. In the midst of making his incredible scientific discoveries, he became drawn to Christianity. Why? The more he discovered and the greater complexity and order he encountered scientifically, the more he sensed the presence of a higher intelligence, the Omnipresence of God. What he ultimately decided for himself only he knows.

Part of the reason for all the different names for God is that, even with all our research, our studies, our experiences, and our understanding of certain aspects, God remains beyond our full comprehension. We all experience God through our unique upbringing, inner soul experiences, wisdom, and heart. Our relationship with God is both universal and deeply personal.

God is everything. Shamanic teacher Llyn Roberts speaks of connecting to our Mother through the Earth. We can ground our energy through direct contact with the soil by walking barefoot, or by sitting with our bottoms on the ground. The Earth can absorb and transmute energy. It's a shame we have become so distant from her. Roberts says, to take the time to observe and feel the life around you. The Earth is sentient, and we have neglected and separated from this important part of us. According to Roberts, we need to synchronize with Mother Earth again, so we do not destroy her, and so we are able to move better into our higher, expanded energetic vibration.

Connecting to the Soul of the Cosmos

With a major reevaluation of our priorities, a restructuring of our way of living, and an effort to raise mass consciousness, can this planet be saved? Connecting to the earth more deeply and healing the physical starts with healing the unseen spiritual. We need to recognize and open ourselves up to the soul and spirit of the cosmos.

The state the world is currently in reflects our disconnect, the results of our past and present priorities, and the choices we have made. We have become blind to what is most important. If we only knew then what we know now. We have no time to waste on regret though. The past is there to reflect on and learn from, so we may change our future. To change the next part of this story, we can't take baby steps. It requires a major paradigm shift. How do we start the needed changes that will improve our lives and heal our planet? We can begin by opening ourselves to deeper, more spiritually attuned lives. Because with that, what brings us joy and the choices we make will naturally change as well.

We are addicted to so many material things, believing that they will make us happy, but they don't. I can relate because when I was a young woman, I fantasized about living in a house the size of a palace, and if anyone had told me then that I shouldn't use shopping as entertainment, I would have thought, "What a stick-in-the-mud. Just let me be." I couldn't feel more differently now!

Where I live, it is difficult to see many of the stars at night. There is too much light noise on the ground from cars, streetlights, houses, and so on. We don't realize how much is being obscured from us until we take a camping trip to the mountains away from any city or town. Once there, when we look up, we are in awe of a sky that is exploding with stars. We suddenly realize what we have been missing. This is similar to the multiple levels of existence, just because we can't see them, doesn't mean they aren't there. We have just lost touch with them. We may feel uncomfortable when we hear an account of someone's spiritual experience beyond the veil. It may not sound believable.

In ancient times people were surrounded by nature, and getting out into nature is still one of the best ways to get in touch with God and Spirit. Many ancient cultures were shamanic, so their relationship with God was more intimate than we are used to now. They visited other realms. Humanity has become distant feeling from God, especially after the removal of our Mother, who is known to be the intermediary between worlds.

As children, we were more innately in touch with God and the spirit realms. I already mentioned the sense of magic I felt outdoors or in the garden in my childhood. I now realize I felt the Holy Spirit there and I sensed other beings. I loved to do drawings and paintings of angels back then. Wonderful things happen when we slow down and find that childlike connection as adults.

What is needed for the world to heal is a different mindset with a radically different set of priorities. It will need to start with us through our personal spiritual journeys, helped along with mindfulness practices such as meditation, prayer, qigong, tai chi, and other practices—including what Mary Magdalene brings forth in her Gospels. Having a practice starts us on a path to incredible joy, meaning, and purpose in life. As the feminine energy is rising on our planet, so is our consciousness. Counterforces can show up too. Stay focused on and believe in the power of the Good.

1 Corinthians 3:16

Know you not, that you are the temple of God
and that the
Spirit of God dwelleth in you?

Spirituality and responsibility go hand in hand. People can believe themselves to be on a spiritual path but are in reality engaging in escapism—going to great lengths to avoid pain and real life! In our quick-fix culture, people can seek shortcuts to spiritual experiences, chasing the highs while avoiding doing the inner work. Such an experience can at times bring about an epiphany that then inspires the inner work, but we cannot avoid the inner work—nor would we want to. Sometimes the greatest transformations can happen at the most painful times in our lives. We will recognize this once we come out the other end. Though rarely completely pain-free, the journey to our higher selves is also incredibly joyful and breathtakingly beautiful.

Wish everyone well on their transformative journeys, including those we perceive as enemies. We don't wish an enemy well in the sense that we allow them to harm us. We absolutely must do what we need to do to keep ourselves safe. But we can wish them well in the sense that we wish for them to heal and grow. That goes for our ex-husbands or ex-wives, even if there is still bad blood between us. The same goes for people of opposing political views and those at the top. We pray for them to transform into their higher selves. It's an important part of our soul's progression to be able to do that. It is also for our own good, as we are all part of the whole.

Once we go deeper within and start our spiritual practices, we feel more responsible for our actions, the welfare of others, and our planet. We start building on a foundation of love and wisdom. For the kind of wisdom that benefits all aspects of life, from the most intimate to the most global, it starts with our own personal spiritual journey, and that's exciting!

Shine Our Light

Matthew 5:14

You are the light of the world.

We have permission to shine our light brightly! Shining our light benefits the world. Too often we shy away from doing so. Partially this can be due to our own fears and partially it can be due to the messages we are getting from some other person or people. There are those who try to dim our light. They make us feel like we have done something wrong for shining. People can do potent damage to us this in way, causing our lives to shrink.

First, we want to make sure that we don't do this to anyone ourselves out of our fears and insecurities. One person's light does not diminish another's. Together, they only transmute the world's darkness to light more effectively.

We do want to make sure we aren't being boastful or conceited, which is unpleasant and will trigger all sorts of reactions. We want to be self-honest regarding what we are displaying. However, be aware that the conceit card can often be used against us, even when we are showing healthy confidence in an effort to keep us small. But do recognize the difference between bragging/conceit and confidence.

Something used to diminish our inner light can come in the form of a seemingly benign comment that isn't benign at all. For example, we can simply radiate confidence when walking into a room, or we can exhibit a gift such as being an incredible singer or great dancer. A remark targeted to subdue our soul light can be subtle or combined with a compliment, such as "You were good out there. I'm not like you though. I don't have the need to draw attention to myself."

Suddenly, having joyfully shared a gift with the world can feel a bit off and needy, and we pull back a little. When this keeps happening, we can pull back a lot.

Our own fears, or unsettling energy directed towards us, especially by someone we love, is another reason we hold back what we have to share with the world. We sub-consciously fear that people will stop loving us if we shine too brightly. Other times the harm can be more direct. with targeted words meant to demoralize and keep us down. Over time, the harm done to our lives can be inconceivable. It can keep a person from contributing to the world what they came here to do. But all of this can only happen if we let it! Become conscious of it, and find a healthy solution.

A qigong teacher shared a story about an experiment. Two plants of the same size were put into separate rooms. For months, when people entered one room they blasted that plant with angry, demeaning words and energy, and in the other room the plant only got words of love and praise. The plant that received the hateful, angry energy, over time, looked sickly and had stunted growth, while the plant that got the love and supportive energy grew plush. Words have energy and power. Hateful energy hurts our souls. According to qigong wisdom, it is even more damaging to our psyche to send hate than to receive it. Watch for these types of toxicity in our lives. With awareness, we can step away or consciously turn things around.

You have permission to shine, in fact, you are being called to shine! Encourage others to do the same! Show us your wonderful personality and your compassionate loving heart; share your gifts; step into your power; expand your light into the world, and shine bright!

What We Do Take with Us

While living on this earthly plane, we can get too caught up in the physical and material. Let's close our eyes, pause, and allow in the awe—that what we see is not all there is! Let's grasp the magnitude of the multiple dimensions of existence! There are worlds within worlds within the cosmos and we are all part of that whole.

Our life here is not an illusion, in the way some people have come to misunderstand it or want to believe it to be. Everything is God or what we call consciousness, and God/consciousness is real—therefore everything is real. The illusion is that of separation.

Our existence here has a great purpose. The lessons we learn or don't learn, the love we feel or the hate we spread, the transformation and growth of our soul—that is what lives on! How we have impacted others, the planet, and who we have become internally stays. Were we compassionate, and did we love deeply or only strive for recognition, wealth, or material gain, never evolving? Anything material eventually crumbles.

The best parents, the brightest leaders, the smartest CEOs, the best teachers, etc., have something in common—they possess an abundance of the kind of knowledge coming from wisdom. Intelligence is a good thing to have as well, but wisdom is by far the most important quality to possess for what matters most—for the welfare of the world and for becoming the highest expression of ourselves. Are we making enough effort to get past all the things keeping us so busy and distracted, to become fully conscious and wise?

What kind of knowledge did we work with while walking this earth? Our actions had consequences—some, we may never realize. Did we work strictly with our intellect and the knowledge of good and evil, or with that of a deep, compassionate wisdom? Humanity gives far too much credit to people with high intelligence who lack wisdom and the results can be seen throughout our planet. Wisdom has compassion; wisdom sees the whole.

If we are starting to realize that we spent our life giving too much attention to the wrong things, it is not too late to change the path of our journey now. Much of what we think is important is just a distraction. We are directed to put so much attention on things—things like money, possessions, and status. Yet, we can't take any of that with us when we leave this reality! Not a thing! What do we take with us? We take with us the evolution of our eternal soul!

The Power of Words and Sound

As mentioned before, the power of words and sounds is underestimated. We are all part of an infinite vibratory field. The vibration of sounds can affect and even reshape us. Words and sounds can heal. Words and sounds can harm. I have heard that victims of physical and emotional abuse will say that both the physical and verbal/emotional abuse were devasting. However, in the cases where their body was able to heal from the physical abuse, the damaging words spoken to them created wounds deep in their hearts and spirits that were harder to mend and come back from. Words and sounds have immense energy.

The Bible opens with the creation of man and woman in God's image, which means gender has meaning and purpose in humanity. Yet, the word to describe all of humankind is "Man". This needs to be healed. For the word man to mean all people makes about as much sense as telling us that God is genderless, yet all persons in the trinity are distinctly identified as male. What visual do we get when we hear the word "man" and what is put out into the vibratory field? We don't see or get the sense of a woman or girl, that's for sure. When we hear the word man, we get the image of a male person. Children most certainly get that image and sense as well. It gives us not only the feeling that men are running the show (and they have been) but it presents men as more genuinely existing and women are just along for the ride, without a true worth or identity of our own. Even most men are baffled that this word hasn't been updated in old material we use frequently, such as old hymns and prayers, considering our current sensibilities and wisdom. It is destructive for that term to still be in material for current use. Because of this, some people are making a conscious effort to correct this language in old material, but a much more far-reaching effort needs to be made.

More of us need to be given a seat at the table. The most inclusive word in the English language is the word "and." When we want to include people at the table, this is the word to use. The blanket word, "man", does not do this.

Now that we understand the great influence of words and their energetic vibrations, we can reflect even more deeply on what was changed and thrown off when our Divine Mother's name and the words describing her were no longer expressed in the world. Even hymns are sung without her in them. Music has a profound effect on the soul.

Speaking of the Holy Spirit as male in the Bible, or even genderless in other writings, sent out not just the misleading words, but a fractured vibratory field. We can only rectify this if we clearly acknowledge "her" again out loud for the feminine being she is, our Divine Mother, the Holy Spirit. We need to bring her back, along with the erased feminine expressions associated with her. Nothing else will rebalance what was thrown off. "Knowing" about her, but without making concrete changes isn't enough. We need to speak of and sing about both our Father God and Mother God, for full acknowledgment, and to fully integrate her energy again here on earth.

The influence of sound is potent. People have healed collapsed lungs and are said to have dissolved tumors with Zhineng Qigong, using sound healing.

Sound healing is done by making long, drawn-out sounds. Each sound correlates with an organ system and its three qualities—physical, emotional, and spiritual. We make these sounds ourselves, so they vibrate in our bodies and by doing this healing can take place!

Giving us back not only our Divine Mother, but the words that made her presence known here on earth is vital, especially now that we know that sound vibrations have even further impact than the meaning of the words alone.

The Power of Meditation, Contemplation and Prayer

With the loss of our Mother, much of the heart and soul of the cosmos went with her. We can now see the signs of the world going through a transformation as she is slowly reemerging. It's time to prepare! We can start by finding quiet time daily to contemplate. We live in a noisy, fast-paced culture, that doesn't give us enough time to reflect, digest, learn, and transform. We can't do this when we are racing through our day. We will find it nearly impossible to get in touch with our higher consciousness in our busy, stressed, outwardly focused existence. When we are in those states of mind we can become cut off from those higher ties. To grow in awareness while also living a more tranquil conscious, connected, wisdom-filled, and purposeful existence, one needs to make the time for stillness and contemplation. Our best tools for this are prayer, mindfulness, meditation, and qigong, which is a moving meditation.

Some form of prayer or meditation is part of all spiritualities and religions, though the way they are expressed can be diverse. That's remarkable. Along with the many benefits of meditation, such as reducing stress, lowering blood pressure, improving physical and mental health, and balancing our emotions, cultivating more empathy, helping us with focus, and being more present—meditation can also open us to the divine and what is beyond this physical reality. This will enhance the quality of our lives in ways we cannot always imagine. Think of the positive shift if we started and ended each day with a gratitude and purpose prayer—"Father, Mother thank you for this day! May I see and appreciate the good and beauty all around me, have the strength to deal with the challenges, enjoy the moment, and contribute where I can." If more people prayed, meditated, practiced qigong, and such, the mass healing and transformation of humanity and the planet would be immeasurable.

Mindfulness and love-centered living are not a New Age concept. Love-centeredness is what Jesus' teachings were based on.

Matthew 22:36-40

> Master, which is the greatest commandment
> in the law? Jesus said to him: Thou shalt
> love the Lord thy God with thy whole heart,
> and with thy whole soul, and with thy
> whole mind. This is the greatest and first
> commandment. And the second is like this:
> Thou shalt love thy neighbor as thyself. On
> these two commandments dependeth the
> whole law and the prophets.

With so much in our digital world polarizing us, disconnecting us from universal love and the cosmos, we need to create space and make it a priority to make time for these practices to start on a conscious path for a more deeply lived and meaningful life.

When I was back home and praying after the opening I experienced at the qigong intensive, I felt such a profound connection and unity with God. Sincere prayer is direct communication with God. The mistake we often make, and which I have been guilty of as well, is we go into autopilot mode. Sometimes we simply recite a memorized prayer without feeling the words. That is not the kind of praying that brings true communion. When we look at the way the Lord's Prayer was translated, a prayer most of us have memorized, not only was our Mother God removed from it, but God is made to feel separate from us: "Our Father who art in Heaven"—The way heaven is often spoken of in religion, it would make us think of the Father God as being up there, and we are down here, when God is actually within us.

Zen Master Thich Nat Hahn expresses how damaging the illusion of separation from God is. He says sincere prayer doesn't need to be heavy, it can be light. Even finding occasional humor in our spiritual quest is a good thing. But what is essential to know when we pray is that God is part of us. We and God do not exist separately. He expresses that the will of God is interconnected to our own will. Feeling that connection while praying is deeply moving. This even gives us hope that if we evolve and change within, sincerely becoming a better person, we can heal our karma. Thich Nat Hahn talks about how when we change the angle of incidence, the angle of reflection will change in that moment.

This interconnection is also found between us and our family. If a parent heals their energy, their children will be positively affected at some level and vice versa. Imagine how this effect can also be extended further to heal the world.

What is encouraged is deep prayer. Deep prayer goes beyond our personal needs, including our needs and wants for our loved ones. Thich Nat Hahn says that the most important thing for us to be able to do is, "to break through the veil of the material plane in order to enter the ultimate dimension and see the interconnection between us and all the phenomena in the world around us."

If we change our consciousness, a global shift in collective consciousness also takes place. If we truly understood our interconnectedness, the divisions between us that are so prevalent in the world right now couldn't exist. The raising of consciousness and world healing can be affected by deep prayer and meditation. The power of prayer is even further amplified when done as a group.

When it comes to meditation, there are so many different types we will want to take time to find what resonates with us. I love both the more classic meditation, as well as Zhineng Qigong. Qigong, which I described as a moving meditation, can be healing on all levels—mind, body, and soul—and can help heal the planet.

Imagine the benefits if we had started meditating earlier in life. This is something that needs to be brought to the schools. An elementary school in Baltimore replaced punishing children with detention or a trip to the principal's office with mindfulness and meditation and saw incredible results. The school reported increased productivity and a healthier learning environment. Not only that, these students are learning skills that will help them throughout life!

My young adult self felt that meditation, yoga, and anything of that nature was a waste of time. I have since discovered that nothing could be further from the truth. There is great power in meditation. When exploring meditation, you will likely come across the talk of a chakra system. Meditation, qigong, and any spiritual practice, including prayer, can start activating your chakras, which is part of raising our consciousness—this is a good thing. The evolution can be very subtle, or it can become powerful. With anything powerful, we want to move forward respectfully and with the proper guidance. We never want to rush things and enjoy the journey.

Some people, after having a spiritual experience or opening can be seduced by illusions of grandeur. It's natural to be excited when something remarkable happens, but if

we start thinking a little too highly of ourselves, it is good to remember the story of Daedalus House. This is the old fable of the man whose cockiness had him flying too high to the sun with wings made of sticks, feathers, and wax—despite being warned it would melt the wax. We all know how that went for him. The moral of the story—is to stay real and stay humble.

Many of the stories in the Bible are not literal, but rather metaphorical. When they say that Mary Magdalene had seven demons expelled from her in the Bible, it is possible they were talking about the seven demons Eastern philosophy talks about that are represented as being at the base of our seven main chakras. Chakras are energy centers along our spine and on top of our head. Blocked or out-of-balance chakras can affect us mentally, physically, emotionally, and spiritually. At the base of each chakra is said to be a demon we need to expel. As we expel them, we are one by one opening the chakras on our way to enlightenment. It is a multifaceted topic that requires research and exploration. In the Gospel of the Beloved Companion, Mary Magdalene describes a similar path to ascension, using a tree symbol with eight levels and seven guardians to overcome to get to the eighth level. So, for Mary Magdalene to have been fully rid of all seven demons/guardians would mean that she was a fully enlightened person!

I should mention that a mistake sometimes made by people seeking enlightenment is to try and rush to the top chakra or experience what is called—the Kundalini awakening—too fast. They are chasing the "ultimate high or ultimate experience" rather than slowly enjoying, savoring every step, and taking in the wisdom of their journey. So much is learned during that time. Getting to the top can take years, decades, or lifetimes. Savor the incredible journey. Experiencing an opening out of sequence or before one is ready and missing those steps in between can cause emotional and mental instability, not enlightenment.

Perhaps simply relaxing, becoming more present, and savoring life's journey by slowing down is our primary goal. Getting off our phones and significantly limiting social media would be an empowering step to take. This can create a lovely shift in consciousness. If we stay at our busy pace, we may never know all we have missed.

I think of the story when Joshua Bell, one of the most gifted violinists of our time, took his several million-dollar Stradivarius violin, donned a t-shirt, and baseball cap and stood in a subway station during rush hour. He played that fine instrument more breathtakingly than most had ever heard in their life. I get goosebumps imagining suddenly coming across music like this while walking through the subway! The idea was to see if people would notice the magnificent talent, the beauty that was sweeping through the station. Would they stop for even a moment to listen? Shockingly, nearly no one did! A child tried to stop, but his mother pulled him away and a man did lean on a wall for a moment. In those 45 minutes, over a thousand people rushed by the mesmerizing music without stopping to listen. How incredibly sad. May we all learn to slow down enough so we don't let life and its beauty pass us by!

Despite the outcome of the Joshua Bell story, I do see a shift taking place. The veil to the other realms is thinning. More people are seeking and becoming conscious of the interconnectedness of life and our being part of something greater. If we keep seeking and raising our awareness, a shift in what we prioritize and how we live life will follow.

The Power of Forgiveness

Forgive others. It benefits our mental and physical health. When we are angry at someone, we can end up sending them damaging energy. This energy has a negative impact on both the receiver and the sender, which can even include losing pieces of the soul. Hate damages the hater the most. Changing our behavior sometimes takes a few tries.

The Bible speaks of forgiveness. Forgiveness can heal a precious relationship. But forgiveness doesn't mean putting ourselves in harm's way by forgetting what happened or that there shouldn't be ramifications, especially if we know the person hasn't changed. Anyone living with an abuser shouldn't feel they deserve the abuse. That's not forgiveness. After making sure we are safe and away from the abuse, and taking whatever proper steps are necessary, forgiveness means letting go of the toxic feelings of anger, resentment, or vengeance towards the person or persons and freeing ourselves. Forgiveness heals us.

Forgiveness seems easier if the offender admits what they did and sincerely apologizes. It is hard to trust someone, even if their behavior has improved some, without the acknowledgment and the apology, for fear that if they don't admit and face what they did, they will likely one day repeat it—sometimes they do so even after apologizing. This concern is understandable. The closeness of the relationship can suffer without the trust more solidly brought back. A sincere apology, along with changed behavior, heals.

Decades ago, I read about the Bemba ethnic group where only the seniors have the right to lecture and criticize a person who does something irresponsible or damaging. The next step for everyone else is to find a time where they all surround the offender and remind them of the good inside of them, by recalling all the wonderful things they have done and contributions they have made. I can only imagine the beautiful character-building and healing this practice brings if it is started early.

We are all human. We've all made mistakes. People make mistakes that range from small to colossal. Everyone has hurt someone intentionally or inadvertently. When an issue comes up, take responsibility for any part we had in the situation, if any. What we must do for our own evolution is stop the lies we tell ourselves about any nasty things we have done and face ourselves squarely, no matter the reason or excuse we may have for having done them. This is a fundamental step for improving our lives. Convincing ourselves that we did nothing wrong is not self-forgiveness; it is escapism. If we have made a mistake, we can reflect on it and allow ourselves to feel what we need to feel. It's better to face it and get through it.

Anytime I realize in hindsight that my actions hurt someone, the person I have always found hardest to forgive is myself. But self-forgiveness is incredibly important. We must forgive ourselves for our own humanness for what we did before we knew better. Then, with our new wisdom, what is vitally important is that we choose to do better! We must remember the good that is inside of us.

We have incarnated here to learn and grow! It is empowering to learn from our mistakes by acknowledging them so we don't repeat them, apologize where it is fit, make amends where possible, and work towards becoming the higher expression of ourselves. To forgive ourselves and forgive others, is to free ourselves and heal.

The Power of Gratitude

With this book, we are encouraged to bring balance back to the cosmos. There is an emotion that can help bring balance back to ourselves. Did you know that gratitude positively changes our brain chemistry?! A *Greater Good* magazine article, "How Gratitude Changes You and Your Brain," published by the Greater Good Science Center at the University of California, Berkeley, states that in their study, those subjects who partook in the act of writing a gratitude letter to someone once a week, compared to those sharing their negative feelings, or those who wrote nothing, showed significant improvement to their mental health and happiness. The benefits of gratitude are felt over time, and they have a lasting, positive effect on our brains! Gratitude can free us from toxic emotions that have previously plagued us. What a gift! Shifting that energy can make it easier for good things to find their way into our lives too! We are more likely to make other people, including our loved ones, feel appreciated, which can have a lovely domino effect.

We don't necessarily need to write down our feelings or put them in a letter—though it is a powerful thing to do at least occasionally. We can simply take time privately at the end of the day to reflect on and notice things such as positive timings or acts of kindness that we didn't take enough note of during the day. Reflecting on those things makes us aware of how much good there is in our lives, even if the day didn't go perfectly or even if we are experiencing hard times. A change in our attitude creates a shift. Gratitude uplifts and unlocks something beautiful. Possessing gratitude while also taking positive action is revitalizing and life-changing. Gratitude helps to heal our brain and can therefore positively shift our circumstances and send healing energy out into the world. Therefore, this is the perfect place to say thank you. I want to take a moment to share my deepest gratitude to every one of you for taking the time out of your life to read what I have written. When starting on this journey I wondered if anyone would be interested in what is being shared. So, a heartfelt thank you! Know that you are precious. I hope and pray that *Holy Spirit Rising* brings profound gifts to your life.

The Greatest is Love

Of all the Bible verses, 1 Corinthians 13:13 is one of my all-time favorites. 1 Corinthians talks about how empty our lives are, no matter what is bestowed upon us, if we don't have love. It talks about how real love isn't jealous or self-seeking and how it is patient and perseveres. In 1 Corinthians 13:13 we learn that of all the spiritual gifts we can be granted whether it be prophecy, whether it be faith, hope or love, though all are treasures—the greatest gift among these is love.

The power of love, our capacity to love and be loved is beyond our logical thinking. It is at the core of our existence. We were born from love. It is what we crave in the depths of our souls yet, in fear, so many of us shut ourselves off to it.

I want to share something I reflect on often that happened many years ago. A friend of mine was standing in a hospital room next to her dying mother. Her mother appeared unconscious, and my friend stood there helpless, knowing in her heart that she was saying her final goodbye. Feeling lost, and not knowing what to do, she turned on the TV in the room and went from channel to channel trying to find something that could hold her attention in her current state of mind. The screen opened to a segment of the talk show Oprah, but she quickly changed the channel and surfed through the other stations. Finding nothing her mind could connect to, she circled back to where she had started with the talk show. She was reaching to turn the TV off when, the host of the show asked her guest, "When someone is on their deathbed, what do they want to know?" My friend's hand froze mid-air. She knew that she was meant to hear this. The guest answered that, no matter whether they are rich or poor, no matter their religion, gender, or ethnicity, when someone is dying what they most want to know is—was I loved and did I love well?

My friend paused, then turned off the TV; she slowly moved toward her mother and took her hand. She gently told her how very much she loved her and how deeply loved she had felt by her. At that moment, she felt her mother's hand give two small squeezes to hers.

At the deepest level of our soul, we are love. It is hard to find love outside ourselves if we don't find it within ourselves first. Recognize this and take positive action if you realize that self-healing is required. You are not alone. Most of us could use some serious self-healing.

We long for love, for love from our mothers, our fathers, families, friends, and we long for romantic love. Due to disappointments, heartbreak, the chaos in the world, and our fears, we start putting up walls to keep ourselves safe, and in doing that, we keep ourselves from the very thing we crave the most. And we are not just talking about romantic love or familial love, we are furthermore talking about love for our fellow human beings. All spiritual work requires a softening and opening of the heart, which will be easier to do with our compassionate Divine Mother's return. Love was at the center of Jesus' teachings, and love is at the center of healing ourselves and the planet.

When we come from a place of love we aren't as competitive towards others in an unhealthy way, always fearing we aren't getting enough, always making comparisons. When we come from that fear-driven place, we hurt, and we hurt others. There is enough for everyone. Release that debilitating fear and step into love. Not everyone will be in that same place with us so navigating the waters of our current world can be tricky.

Was I loved and did I love well? If that is our dying question—if that is what matters most—what do we need to change in our priorities today to make love our focus; so that when the time comes our answer to that question is a resounding—yes!

The Prophecy

When I was checking on the internet to see if any other book already had the title, *Holy Spirit Rising*, I came across a low-budget documentary with the title *Shekinah Rising*. In the documentary they mostly talked about the Hasidic Jewish way of life for women. Then there was a lovely moment where they shared the ancient Hasidic prophecy that says that before the Messiah comes, the Shekinah, the feminine aspect of God must rise, and that women will lead the way into the new era! I was overcome with emotion upon hearing those words, because I already knew this in my heart, and we are already starting to see the truth of that prophecy emerging!

Conclusion:
All Together Now: Global Evolution

A dramatic societal paradigm change needs to take place. If we stay as polarized as we are now, humanity won't make it. What we are leaving for our kids to deal with, the young generation, is unconscionable. We are better than this. We are at a critical planetary turning point, and getting through it requires collaboration across the board at a global level. We need to get those at the top to see that healing our planet needs to be their highest focus above all else. What this requires then, is a dramatic shift in priorities and the raising of mass consciousness. We must come together with a common goal—to save the planet and humanity's future. All the destruction, division, and strife are not in line with our true nature. We are heading to times of unprecedented collaboration and healing.

Did you know that World War I, one of the deadliest global battles in history, was nearly brought to an end by the spontaneous Christmas Truces of 1914? Historian Stanley Weintraub, author of *Silent Night*, wrote about these truces. Many happened in various areas across the front, during an agreed upon Christmas cease-fire.

In one story he shared, a soldier in the trench on one side started singing "Silent Night/Stille Nacht". Though the language was different, the opposing side recognized the melody and started chiming in and singing in their respective language, while occasionally joking and sending insults to each other. The energy shifted—the soldiers of two opposing sides were now singing a heartfelt "Silent Night, Stille Nacht" in perfect unison. That's when it happened—first, there was one—a young German soldier slowly walked towards the center of no-man's land with a white flag and a small Christmas tree in hand. As he stood there, more soldiers joined him. They at first hesitantly then spontaneously put down their weapons of hand-to-hand combat to emotionally bury their dead and pay their respects to the fallen on both sides. The boys and men started talking as best they could and then challenged each other to a spontaneous game of soccer.

The truce and the games went on for the duration of the holiday cease-fire. Soldiers from both sides exchanged wine and chocolates and traded treats that had been sent from home. During the games, they joked around with one another and discovered that they liked each other.

Stanley Weintraub shared an instance where an English soldier met his former barber, a German who used to live in London before the war. The English soldier complained that he hadn't gotten a good haircut since the other guy left. The German soldier said he had his scissors with him and set up a makeshift stool and the English soldier had his haircut by the German right there on the battlefield! Think of the integrity and trust that was required of both men for this moment to have gone well.

When it came time to fight again, no one wanted to be the first one to shoot toward the friends they'd made, wondering whose life they would end, whose family they would destroy with their bullet. The propaganda smoke screen from the top had been lifted. They had seen that these boys and men weren't their foes. They weren't any different than them. They had seen the humanity in each other.

It was a serious dilemma because when the cease-fire was over the soldiers refused to fight. When forced to shoot, both sides were shooting into the air to avoid hitting anybody. Some troops needed to be sent home and replaced, others were forced to keep fighting with the threat that if they didn't, they would be court-martialed or shot. None of those soldiers were ever the same again, after the legendary Christmas Truces of 1914, that nearly ended a World War.

My Mystical Vision:
We Are One with God

I have chosen to keep most of my spiritual experiences out of public discussion because they feel intimate and private to me. In closing, however, there is one experience I feel compelled to share because of how it can uplift us all and put an end to the false sense of separation we have believed in for too long. When I had a series of spontaneous shamanic experiences, this was the final and biggest one during that time.

In the wee hours of the morning, I was awakened. I was awake and alert but had my eyes closed. It was so early that the physical world was still not fully lit. Suddenly the entire world, the entire cosmos went bright, luminescent, energetic white, and I saw the interconnection of all things. I cannot describe the experience or feeling with mere words. The white had energy and almost a rolling movement to it, with a look of dense, gently vibrating molecules. There was no space between them as they rolled and moved in breathtaking beauty. I was still me consciously, yet I was seamlessly immersed in this Great White. There was no physical shape, border, or separation between the energetic presence and my energetic presence. I was all of it, and it was all of me. I was part of everything. Everyone and everything there is, was in this whole. There was nothing, no one in the cosmos not fully submerged in the whole, in the All.

Overwhelmed with awe, I felt I was in the presence of God. We all are. And God is pure, pure love. I was moved to tears. When my eyes finally opened, all I continued to feel was this indescribable love. I walked around for days feeling nothing but love for everything in such a complete way I had never felt before, for everyone that exists, existed, and will exist, whether perceived as friend or foe—everything in existence—trees, birds, everything felt like it was permeated with the love coming from within me and all around me. Though I seek to become this unconditional love once again, I knew the feeling wasn't going to last at this time for me because I still had work to do, and in the state I was in, I may not go about it the way necessary, with what is currently going on in the world. However, some of that unconditional love did remain with me and the experience changed my life, my aspirations, and my consciousness forever.

What different values, goals, perceptions, understanding, and feelings we would have if we knew God and each other this way—if we cherished our connection, our ultimate oneness with God, and lived in a manner that reflected that? We are all part of God. Everything is God and God is love beyond our wildest imagination!

References and Valuable Resources for Further Reading

Here I share what I have read over the last few years. I did not receive money for listing these books, films, and articles here. I simply added whatever I have read and felt were well-researched, valuable resources others could benefit from. They contain incredible investigative work, intelligence, insight, and wisdom. I don't always agree with every view or detail, and likely neither will you, but I resonate with much of the wisdom shared and appreciate the contributions to humanity made by the authors.

Just as in early Christianity, there are differences of opinion. Even among these authors, there are variations. Some authors had additional insights later in life, as more information became available to them. They may have in earlier writings given to Mary the mother of Jesus, some of what they now attribute to Mother God, for example. The authors also may not agree on important details, but they share the mission of bringing wisdom and healing to the world through their insights.

While exploring, be patient with yourself and allow yourself time. The absorption of this multifaceted, transformational material can take a while. It can take years. I always read and then reflect on it and live with it for a while. I keep exploring as I am ready, taking breaks in between.

Many of these books and resources are online for free or can be found at the library, including the online library app for your area. If not carried by your local library, many can be requested and borrowed from another library.

Some of the videos here can be found for free on Kanopy.com, Vimeo, or YouTube. The articles and talks are found free online. I also include a random list of conscious media films I've watched, as examples of how broad and fun the range is. This is a minuscule sampling of films and documentaries found on various entertainment platforms to give us a sense of what constitutes conscious media.

Enjoy your journey!

A Book by This Author for Children

Dorme: A Magical Dreamland Visit
by Sylvia Binsfeld
ConsciousMediaMovement.org

Books

Christian Books on Mother Holy Spirit

Finding Holy Spirit Mother by Ally Kateusz

Our Mother the Holy Spirit by Marianne Widmalm

Great High Priest: The Temple Roots of Christian Liturgy by Margaret Barker

The Meaning of Ruah at Qumran by Arthur Everett Sekki

More Books on the Divine Feminine

The Divine Feminine: The Biblical Imagery as God as Female by Virginia Ramey Mollenkott

The Feminine Spirit at the Heart of the Bible by Lynne Bundesen

The Divine Feminine by Anne Baring and Andrew Harvey

Myth of the Goddess by Anne Baring and Jules Cashford

The Divine Feminine in Biblical Wisdom Literature by Rabbi Rami Shapiro

Book on the Kabbalah

Introduction to the World of Kabbalah by Z'ev ben Shimon Halevi

Books on the Gnostic Gospels

Gnostic Gospels by Elaine Pagels

The Gospel of the Beloved Companion: The Complete Gospel of Mary Magdalene translated by Jehanne de Quillan

The Gospel of Thomas by Elaine Pagels

The Gnostic Gospel of Philip, translation and annotation by Andrew Phillip Smith

Books on Adam and Eve

Temple Theology: An Introduction by Margaret Barker. (Book on the Old Testament, includes Adam and Eve)

Adam Eve and the Serpent by Elaine Pagels

Books on Mary Magdalene

Mary Magdalene, The First Apostle: The Struggle for Authority by Ann Graham Brock

The Gospel of Mary of Magdala: Jesus and the First Woman Apostle by Karen King

The Meaning of Mary Magdalene: Discovering the Woman at the Heart of Christianity by Cynthia Bourgeault

Mary Magdalene Revealed by Meggan Watterson

Book on Sarah: The Prophet

Sarah the Priestess: The First Matriarch of Genesis by Savina Teubal

Book on the Lord's Prayer

Prayers of the Cosmos: Reflecting the Original Meaning of Jesus's Words by Neil Douglas-Klotz

The Inclusive Bible

If you look at the long list of contributors to the popular versions of the Bible, you will likely not be surprised to find an all-male line-up. With so many qualified women translators, we would hope for some balance in gender in the contributors. The inclusive version of the Bible has both female and male contributors.

The Inclusive Bible: The First Egalitarian Translation by Priests for Equality

Book Celebrating the Commonalities in Religions

The Mystic Vision by Anne Baring and Andrew Harvey

Books: Spiritual Growth Resources

Though many meditation books and such aren't written by Christians, they teach along the same lines as what Jesus taught in the many gospels. Jesus was a mystic. Numerous scholars feel that the missing Jesus years, that period between late childhood and age 29, where nothing was documented about him, were years he spent learning from the masters. Some speculate he went to India and/or Tibet, others that he studied with the Essenes. Others simply believe he worked as a carpenter in Galilee for part of that time.

For our own spiritual work, the type of meditation and other practices we choose will be personal and unique to us, usually learning by trial and error or what we are intuitively drawn to. The books below teach inner peace and mindful living. Meditation raises our awareness around our unity and can open us to wisdom and a higher way of being. Mindfulness paired with positive action can help heal us and the world.

After that, we can find a variety of material that will raise our awareness.

Books on Meditation, Mindfulness and Spiritual Practice

Follow Your Breath: A Foundational Technique by Sharon Salzberg (audio)

Embracing Your Boundless Heart by Sharon Salzberg (audio)

The Miracle of Mindfulness: An Introduction to the Practice of Meditation by Thich Nhat Hanh

Meditation for Beginners by Jack Kornfield

Zhineng (Chilel) Qigong: Overview and Foundation Methods by Hou Hee Chan

A Culture of Happiness: How to Scale Up Happiness from People to Organizations by Tho Ha Vinh

Eye of the Heart by Cynthia Bourgeault

The Good Remembering by Llyn Roberts

Books on Planetary Healing

Soul Power: An Agenda for a Conscious Humanity by Anne Baring and Dr. Scilla Elworthy

Spiritual Ecology: The Cry of the Earth by Llewellyn Vaughan-Lee

Limits and Beyond: 50 years on from The Limits to Growth, what did we learn and what's next? by Ugo Bardi and Carlos Alvarez Pereira

Books on Peace Building

Tools For Peace by Scilla Elworthy

A Business Plan for Peace by Scilla Elworthy

Books on Natural Healing

The Flower Essence Repertory by Patricia Kaminski and Richard Katz

Hildegard of Bingen's Holistic Health Secrets by Melanie Schmidt-Ulmann

The Nutritionist's Kitchen by Carly Knowles

Books I Have Not Read, but Plan to Soon!

I always have an active stack of books piling up. Since I haven't read the books below, I don't have an opinion on them yet.

The Great Lady: Restoring her Story by Margaret Barker

Mary Magdalene Unveiled by Annine van der Meer

The Gnostic Paul: Gnostic Exegesis of the Pauline Letters by Elaine Pagels

Qigong Zhengti Therapy by Michelle Treseler and Teacher Ning (coming soon)

Merchants of Light by Betty J. Kovacs

Sacred Economics by Charles Eisenstein

Invisible Women by Caroline Crado Perez

Post Growth: Life After Capitalism by Tim Jackson

Scholarly Biblical Talks

Mary Magdalene by Anne Baring
https://www.youtube.com/watch?v=kDclP5aDgaM

The Holy Spirit by Jack Levinson
https://youtu.be/eqvyjtBAGos

The Gospel of Mary by Elaine Pagels
https://www.youtube.com/watch?v=4lqQshEzE00

Gnostic God vs Orthodox God by Elaine Pagels
https://www.youtube.com/watch?v=5h52beXavf8

Adam and Eve by Anne Baring
https://www.youtube.com/watch?v=P1JLWWo9l-w&t=15s

A Walk Through the Old Testament by Margaret Barker
Includes Story of Adam and Eve

Part #1
https://youtu.be/P-McdWooM9Y

Part #2
https://www.youtube.com/watch?v=ZJ9kjWt_L_8

Part #3
https://www.youtube.com/watch?v=yduuTRVqoTg

Part #4
https://www.youtube.com/watch?v=lKzECtLpurY

Websites, Articles, Video Talks

Feminine Holy Spirit

The Wisdom Texts: Divine Wisdom, Sophia, Holy Spirit by Anne Baring
https://www.anne-baring.com/anbar08_seminar13.htm

The Mother of God's People by Rev. Dr. Craig Atwood
https://www.jstor.org/stable/3170208

The Holy Spirit is Female! by Rev. Dcn. David Justin Lynch
https://saintceciliacatholiccommunity.org/blog/the-holy-spirit-is-female/

Academia: Holy Spirit as the Mother of the Son
https://www.academia.edu/44608100/The_Holy_Spirit_as_the_Mother_of_the_Son_Origen_s_Interpretation_Of_a_Surviving_Fragment_from_the_Gospel_According_to_the_Hebrews

Woman, Wisdom and The Word: Reflections on the Divine Feminine
https://twotreesinthegarden.com/2024/02/04/woman-wisdom-and-the-word-reflections-on-the-divine-feminine/

Blasphemy of St. Augustine by James Hale
https://philosophynow.org/issues/35/The_Blasphemy_of_Saint_Augustine

What Became of God the Mother? by Elaine Pagels
https://womenpriests.org/sexuality/pagels-what-became-of-god-the-mother/

Holy Spirit Mother, the Baptismal Womb, and the Walesby Tank by Ally Kateutz
https://allykateusz.org/wp-content/uploads/2023/01/Holy_Spirit_Mother_the_Baptismal_Womb_an.pdf

Motherhood of Holy Spirit in 18th Century by Rev. Dr. Craig Atwood
https://theflamingheretic.wordpress.com/2011/04/08/motherhood-of-holy-spirit-in-18th-century/

The Holy Spirit as feminine: Early Christian testimonies and their interpretation: Johannes van Oort
http://www.scielo.org.za/pdf/hts/v72n1/26.pdf

Deidre Havrelock Website with posts on the Holy Spirit & Adam and Eve
https://www.deidrehavrelock.com

Gnostic Gospels

Story of the Storytellers: The Gnostic Gospels (Frontline) by Elaine Pagels
https://www.pbs.org/wgbh/frontline/article/gnostic-gospels

Women Leaders

Women Leadership in the Moravian Church by Rev. Dr. Craig Atwood
https://theflamingheretic.wordpress.com/2011/09/14/women-leadership-in-the-moravian-church/

Junia Gets a Sex Change by Robin Cohn
https://robincohn.net/junia-gets-a-sex-change/

Phoebe: A Diakonos by Claude Mariottini
https://claudemariottini.com/2009/09/26/phoebe-a-diakonos/

Junia, a Female Apostle: An Examination of the Historical Record by CBE
https://www.cbeinternational.org/resource/article/priscilla-papers-academic-journal/junia-female-apostle-examination-historical

A Reexamination of Phoebe as a "Diakonos" and "Prostatis": Exposing the Inaccuracies of English Translations by Elizabeth McCabe
https://www.sbl-site.org/publications/article.aspx?ArticleId=830

Early Christian Women
https://allykateusz.org/

Mary Magdalene

Video: Who Framed Mary Magdalene? Mixed-Genre/Documentary 30 minutes
https://youtu.be/aSFf1NjQnQ4

The Gospel of Mary of Magdala: Jesus and the First Woman Apostle by Karen King
http://www.gnosis.org/library/GMary-King-Intro.html

What is Truth? by Jerry Kennell
https://twotreesinthegarden.com/2016/11/27/what-is-truth/

Mary Magdalene: Consort of Jesus and Apostle to the Apostles by Anne Baring
https://www.anne-baring.com/anbar60_marymagdalene.html

Duke Today: Bible Edits that Downplay Mary Magdalene Mary or Martha?: A Duke scholar's research finds Mary Magdalene downplayed by New Testament scribes by Eric Ferreri
https://today.duke.edu/2019/06/mary-or-martha-duke-scholars-research-finds-mary-magdalene-downplayed-new-testament-scribes

Cambridge University Press|
Was Martha of Bethany Added to the Fourth Gospel in the Second Century? by Elizabeth Schrader
https://www.cambridge.org/core/journals/harvard-theological-review/article/abs/was-martha-of-bethany-added-to-the-fourth-gospel-in-the-second-century/6CBD2C9576A583DD02987FE836C427B7

Adam and Eve

The Dangerous Couple: The Story of Adam and Eve By Anouar Majid
https://www.tingismagazine.com/editorials/a-dangerous-couple-the-story-of-adam-and-eve/

Feminine and Masculine Principles

Feminine and Masculine Principles by Center for Action and Contemplation
https://cac.org/feminine-and-masculine-principles-2018-04-22/

Misrepresentation of Apostle Paul

Paul, a First Century Feminist by Rev. Dr. Jeffrey Frantz
https://progressivechristianity.org/resources/paul-a-first-century-feminist/

Destructive Power of One Mistranslated Word

What a Difference a Word Can Make by Paul Ellis
https://escapetoreality.org/2021/02/18/what-1-corinthians-14-26/

Immaculate Conception and Church Doctrine

Immaculate Conception Became Catholic Doctrine by Diana Severance, Ph.D.
https://www.christianity.com/church/church-history/timeline/1801-1900/immaculate-conception-became-catholic-doctrine-11630497.html

Current Day Impact

Working Towards Gender Equality

Better World for my Daughter
https://goodmenproject.com/featured-content/i-want-a-better-world-for-my-daughter-how-can-i-convince-other-men-to-care/

Video Talk: Natalie Portman on Empowering Women & Girls Everywhere
https://www.youtube.com/watch?v=7ZPDXNrtNsM

Women's issues at UN: Still 'too low down on the agenda'
https://apnews.com/article/virus-outbreak-beijing-international-news-womens-rights-united-nations-general-assembly-3cfdfd897a076a5488bfca857c51b0e3

Teaching Women's History: The Marginalization of Women
https://www.nyhistory.org/blogs/teaching-womens-history-marginalization-of-womenmarginalization-of-women

Men and Masculinity: How Toxic Masculinity Hurts Mental Health
https://goodmenproject.com/everyday-life-2/men-and-masculinity-how-toxic-masculinity-hurts-mental-health-auth/

Women Who Had Their Work Stolen by Men
https://historycollection.com/women-who-had-their-work-stolen-from-them-by-men/

Harvard Business: "Lean In" Messages and the Illusion of Control
https://hbr.org/2018/07/lean-in-messages-and-the-illusion-of-control +

CBE International (Christians for women's equality. Members may not ascribe to a female Holy Spirit)
https://www.cbeinternational.org/resource/article/mutuality-blog-magazine/setting-stage-equality-welcoming-womens-voices-christian

Equality Increases Length of Life for Both Genders
https://journals.plos.org/globalpublichealth/article?id=10.1371/journal.pgph.0001214

Women and Girls in Film and Television

Study shows how women directors get blocked in Hollywood
https://fortune.com/2015/10/06/women-directors-hollywood/

Geena Davis Institute on Gender in Media
https://www.SeeJane.org

The Wrap: 'I'll Never Let Any Woman Direct Me
https://www.thewrap.com/11-women-directors-hollywood-sexism-gender-bias-female-discrimination/

Britannica: Alice-Guy Blanche
https://www.britannica.com/biography/Alice-Guy-Blache

Women in Film Equal Pay Issues

Equal Pay on Sets
https://www.biography.com/movies-tv/suzanne-somers-threes-company-equal-pay

Video Talk: Natalie Portman's Guide to Toppling the Patriarchy (Her talk before Weinstein's arrest)
https://youtu.be/0qukNm3Bhgg?si=iIQm9bq6r-yuTX7N

Michelle Williams Felt 'Paralyzed' After Learning of Pay Gap Between Her and Co-Star Mark Wahlberg
https://www.usatoday.com/story/life/people/2019/04/02/michelle-williams-felt-paralyzed-over-mark-wahlberg-pay-gap-news/3345072002/

Marriage and Relationships

BYU Equal Partnership in Marriage
https://foreverfamilies.byu.edu/equal-partnership-in-marriage

The Marriage Lesson That I Learned Too Late
https://www.theatlantic.com/family/archive/2022/04/marriage-problems-fight-dishes/629526

Women and Medicine

Dying to be Heard
https://www.usnews.com/news/the-report/articles/2018-04-20/why-women-struggle-to-get-doctors-to-believe-them

Dismissed
https://www.today.com/health/dismissed-health-risk-being-woman-t153804

Big Pharma Is Hijacking the Information Doctors Need Most
https://time.com/6171999/big-pharma-clinical-data-doctors/

Saving Our Planet

For Humanity and the Planet to Thrive, We Need to Empower Women
https://www.clubofrome.org/blog-post/earth4all-empowerment/

Youth Activism
https://mashable.com/article/youth-activism-2023-so-far

I'm a Climate Scientist Who Believes in God. Hear Me Out
https://www.nytimes.com/2019/10/31/opinion/sunday/climate-change-evangelical-christian.html

From Equality to Sustainability PDF
https://www.clubofrome.org/publication/earth4all-inequality-to-sustainability/

PLOS Emissions Report
https://journals.plos.org/climate/article?id=10.1371/journal.pclm.0000190

To Fight Climate Despair, this Christian Ecologist Says Science isn't Enough
https://www.washingtonpost.com/religion/2022/04/16/climate-despair-christian-scientist-finding-hope/

America's Richest 10% are Responsible for 40% of its Planet-Heating Pollution, New Reports Find

CNN:
https://www.cnn.com/2023/08/17/business/rich-americans-climate-footprint-emissions/index.html

FOX:
https://fox59.com/news/national-world/40-percent-of-us-climate-emissions-attributed-to-richest-households-study/

Cassandra, Consumption and Callings
https://cylviahayes.substack.com/p/cassandra-consumption-and-callings?utm_source=substack&utm_medium=emai

A Crutial Time of Choice
https://www.annebaring.com/a-crucial-time-of-choice/

What an Ecological System Looks Like
https://www.yesmagazine.org/issue/ecological-civilization/2021/02/16/what-does-ecological-civilization-look-like

Economist Says Our Obsession With Growth Must End
https://www.nytimes.com/interactive/2022/07/18/magazine/herman-daly-interview.html

Quality of Life Not GDP Should Be Our Measure of Success.
https://thecorrespondent.com/357/outgrowing-growth-why-quality-of-life-not-gdp-should-be-our-measure-of-success

Louisiana's Rising Sea Levels
https://www.pbs.org/newshour/nation/difficult-conversations-how-rising-sea-levels-threaten-the-lives-of-louisianas-coastal-residents

Peace: A World Without Violence

Video: Scilla Elworthy: Business Plan for Peace
https://www.youtube.com/watch?v=vH1WgurH5FA

'It's a Moral Issue.' Gun Control Activist David Hogg
https://www.calpoly.edu/news/its-moral-issue-gun-control-activist-david-hogg-speaks-cal-poly

Women and War: Securing a More Peaceful Future
https://www.wilsoncenter.org/event/women-and-war-securing-more-peaceful-future

Study Shows Women Leaders Get Backlash for Pursuing Peace
https://www.cmu.edu/dietrich/news/news-stories/2023/december/schwartz-leadership.html

More Women Leaders Won't Lead to More Peace (*Peace will be a challenge while there is still gender discrimination)
https://www.lawfaremedia.org/article/why-more-female-leaders-won-t-lead-to-more-peace

Empowering Female Leadership in Times of Global Challenges
https://clubofrome.podbean.com/e/empowering-female-leadership-in-times-of-global-challenges/

Science and Religion

Darwin vs God
https://dennisklocek.com/darwin-vs-god/

Science of God
https://www.washingtonpost.com/wpsrv/newsweek/science_of_god/scienceofgod.htm

The World is not an Illusion
https://www.psychologytoday.com/intl/blog/out-the-darkness/201704/the-world-is-not-illusion

Conscious Business and Economics

Transforming Business
https://weall.org/transforming-business

A Healthy Economy Should be Designed to Thrive, Not Grow
https://youtu.be/Rhcrbcg8HBw?si=8BoYhA6m2ks6oztx

Video Talk: Economic Reality Check
https://www.ted.com/talks/tim_jackson_an_economic_reality_check

Conscious Media Movement Blog: Sacred Economics with Cylvia Hayes
https://www.consciousmediamovement.org/single-post/sacred-eco-nomics-with-cylvia-hayes

Planetary Turnaround: an investment banker's perspective on climate change action
https://www.clubofrome.org/wp-content/uploads/2022/05/Earth4All_Deep_Dive_Lake_Randers.pdf

Population Growth

A Declining World Population isn't Catastrophe: It Could Actually Some Bring Good
https://www.washingtonpost.com/opinions/2021/06/07/please-hold-panic-about-world-population-decline-its-non-problem/

Why Declining Birth Rates are Good News for Life on Earth
https://www.theguardian.com/commentisfree/2021/jul/08/why-declining-birth-rates-are-good-news-for-life-on-earth

Articles on Bringing Mother Nature to Cities

Study on Neighborhood Greenery's Effect on Crime Rate
https://www.ncbi.nlm.nih.gov/pmc/articles/PMC7084215/

The Infrastructure Law's Untapped Potential for Promoting Community Safety
https://www.brookings.edu/blog/the-avenue/2022/03/29/the-infrastructure-laws-untapped-potential-for-promoting-community-safety/

Importance of Spending Time in Nature

Nurtured by Nature
https://www.apa.org/monitor/2020/04/nurtured-nature

Couch Potatoes Beware
*https://www.acc.org/about-acc/press-releases/2011/01/12/11/5
1/011011screentimeheartrisks*

Mental Health

Student Mental Health is in Crisis
*https://www.apa.org/monitor/2022/10/mental-health-
campus-care*

Dangers of Sleep Deprivation
*https://med.stanford.edu/news/all-news/2015/10/among-
teens-sleep-deprivation-an-epidemic.html*

Video: "Don't Tell Me to just Breath"-Meditation+Action
https://www.youtube.com/watch?v=R4IFM2iZgbk

Issues With Social Media

Wasting Your Life on Social Media
*https://cinziadubois.medium.com/youre-wasting-your-life-on-
social-media-3606058cac87*

Lawsuits Pile Up as Parents Take on Social Media Giants
*https://www.context.news/big-tech/long-read/lawsuits-
pile-up-as-us-parents-take-on-social-media-giants?utm_
source=pocket-newtab*

Teenage Social Media Use Linked to Less Life-Satisfaction for
Some
https://www.bbc.com/news/health-60875884

Social Media Can Threaten Your Time, Mental Health, and Life
Goals
*https://ultratechlife.com/blog/social-media-time-wasting-
mental-health-tips/*

Scientific Study: Is "Snapchat Dysmorphia" a Real Issue
https://www.ncbi.nlm.nih.gov/pmc/articles/PMC5933578/

Women's Self-Objectification and Strategic Self-Presentation on Social Media
https://journals.sagepub.com/doi/ full/10.1177/03616843221143751

Mindfulness and Meditation

Video: Christian Centering Prayer
https://www.youtube.com/watch?v=1aQmQu4lufo&t=1713s

How To/Enjoy Sitting Meditation (See book section for more samples)
https://plumvillage.org/articles/enjoy-sitting-meditation/

Mindfulness Can Literally Change Your Brain
https://hbr.org/2015/01/mindfulness-can-literally-change-your-brain

How Gratitude Changes You and Your Brain
https://greatergood.berkeley.edu/article/item/how_ gratitude_changes_you_and_your_brain

What Happens When Meditation Replaces School Detention
https://ptaourchildren.org/meditation-not-detention/
https://www.cnn.com/2016/11/04/health/meditation-in-schools-baltimore/index.html

Video Talk: Energy Healing and Medical Qigong

Video: *Medical Qigong Healing*
https://www.monroeinstitute.org/blogs/podcasts/energy-healing-with-lisa-van-ostrand-dr-of-medical-qigong

Video: *Saving Kelli with Wisdom Healing Qigong* (Zhineng)
https://www.youtube.com/watch?v=RIEfF1iZfUo

Video: *Lift Chi Up, Pull Chi Down Qigong Practice*
https://www.youtube.com/watch?v=YNujpRnLtWU&t=179s

Benefiting from the Wisdom of Our Elders

Cooperation vs Ageism
https://www.consciousmediamovement.org/single-post/2017/10/24/coming-soon-ageism-vs-cooperation

Wise Elders Needed in Business And Technology
https://www.theatlantic.com/family/archive/2022/03/older-workers-silicon-valley-business/623880/?utm_source=pocket-

The Human Library

The Human Library
https://humanlibrary.org/

Saving Our Planet Websites and Organizations

Club of Rome
https://www.clubofrome.org

Bioneers:
https://bioneers.org/

Wellbeing Economy Alliance
https://weall.org/?utm_source=substack&utm_medium=email

The Rethink
https://www.therethink.org/

Rights of Nature
https://www.garn.org/?utm_source=substack&utm_medium=email

Fiber Systems that Build Soil & Protect Our Biosphere
https://fibershed.org/

Regenerative Agriculture
https://nfu.org/2020/10/12/the-indigenous-origins-of-regenerative-agriculture/

The Conscious Media Movement
https://www.ConsciousMediaMovement.org

Public Speaking for Women

KC Baker: Women Speak: Find your voice
https://womanspeak.com

Videos

Note: This book aims to be politically party-neutral. Though I have always been more spiritual than political, the two intersect. We want to be conscious in both arenas. I've included documentaries made by a filmmaker who is married to a political figure and a one made by celebrities. They can be watched on platforms such as Netflix, Prime, Kanopy, etc. Due to the great division in the U.S. at the time of this writing, it concerned me that including them would be viewed as a political statement. It is not meant as such. They were simply the best films on the topic I could currently find. We talk about our oneness in this book. We can only heal the planet by seeing the humanity in each other. One of the disadvantages of division is that we miss out on each other's contributions, wisdom, friendships, and so much more that would make the world a better place. I felt it was important to share these incredible documentaries on their respective topics.

As mentioned before, I have also included a random list of entertaining conscious media feature films I've enjoyed watching, as examples of how broad and fun the conscious media range is. This is a minuscule sampling of films and documentaries to give us a sense of what kind of stories would be considered conscious media. It was tempting to add others, but I had to make myself stop.

When looking through titles to make some quick choices, I found that a few films have the right idea but are presented in a way that makes it harder for many people to relate to them. The ambitious film *Cloud Atlas* has so much to say, especially regarding how our individual choices have far-reaching consequences, sometimes past our lifetime. However, it was difficult for me to follow all the storylines and the characters felt distant and disconnected from me. I wish that weren't so because in many ways, it was a spectacular movie, and I loved the message. I got more out of it the second time viewing it. It could be worth a watch.

Enjoy discovering wonderful movies on your own! Film and story have such an impact on our lives! It's empowering to be aware of it and watch consciously.

Documentaries

Women's Issues
Misrepresentation

Men's Issues
The Mask You Live In

Sexual Violence
The Hunting Ground College

Sexual Violence at the Schools

Women in Film
This Changes Everything/Geena Davis Institute

Race and Class
Hoop Dreams

Social Media Exposed
The Social Dilemma

Food Consciousness
Food, Inc.

We Are What We Eat

More Than Honey

The Beauty of Nature

A Life on Our Planet

Fantastic Fungi

Nature/ Saving Our Planet
Kiss the Ground

Chasing Coral

The Year the Earth Changed/ David Attenborough

2040

Flint: The Poisoning of a City

Common Ground

Day Zero

The Biggest Little Farm

Stewart Udall: The Politics of Beauty

Wild Life (2023)

Blackfish

Virunga

Remothering the Land: (Free short film)
https://vimeo.com/662833500

Feature Films

Don't Look Up

Killers of the Flower Moon

Brooklyn

A Beautiful Mind

Whale Rider

Moana

The Shawshank Redemption

Won't You Be My Neighbor

Hidden Figures

It's a Wonderful Life

Lord of the Rings

Erin Brockovich

Little Women

The Killing Fields

Children of Heaven: Foreign language

The Color of Paradise: Foreign language

My Year of Living Mindfully

Moonlight

She Said

Peaceful Warrior

The Quiet Girl

Bombshell

The Breakfast Club

The Shape of Water

Boys Don't Cry

Babette's Feast-Foreign language

A Man Called Otto

Legally Blonde

RGB

Mystic River

The Book Thief

Indochine

Avitar

Films for Children

Moana

Rudolph the Red-Nosed Reindeer

The Boy, the Mole, the Fox, and the Horse

Spirited Away

The Chronicles of Narnia: The Lion, the Witch and the Wardrobe

A Charlie Brown Christmas

E.T. The Extra-Terrestrial

Anne of Green Gables

Luca

Inside Out

Babe

Kiki's Delivery Service

The Elephant Queen

Toy Story

Kung Fu Panda 3

The Lorax

Akeelah and the Bee

Powerful Free Videos

Who Framed Mary Magdalene? Mixed-Genre/Documentary 30 min.
https://youtu.be/aSFf1NjQnQ4

Shekinah Rising Trailer: This link is to a free trailer that speaks of that ancient prophecy regarding the Shekinah we had discussed earlier. The low-budget documentary itself, on the Hassidic Jewish women's way of life, is not free.
https://vimeo.com/387560025

Scilla Elworthy: Business Plan for Peace Talk
https://www.youtube.com/watch?v=vH1WgurH5FA

Scilla Elworthy -Discovering the Power of your Heart
https://www.youtube.com/watch?v=4k28k4AGiWI

Economic Reality Check
*https://www.ted.com/talks/tim_jackson_an_economic_*
reality_check

Natalie Portman's Guide to Toppling the Patriarchy (Her talk
before Weinstein's arrest)
https://youtu.be/0qukNm3Bhgg?si=iIQm9bq6r-yuTX7N

Natalie Portman on Empowering Women & Girls Everywhere
https://www.youtube.com/watch?v=7ZPDXNrtNsM

Don't Tell Me to Just Breath
https://youtu.be/0RPARLsVHHU?si=IP3Cm6JCBzWfEn_3

Healing the Economy, Healing the Planet, Healing Our Mental
Health
https://www.youtube.com/watch?v=R4IFM2iZgbk

Credit for Historical Images

The Immaculate Conception Section Image

Credit: The Virgin and Child being crowned by angels, and
above them are God the Father and the dove of the Holy Spirit.
Photo reproduced lithograph. Welcome Collection. Public
Domain Mark Photo reproduced lithograph. Reference 30743i

Holy Trinity Fresco Art in St. Jakobus Chapel

Wikimedia Creative Commons Public Domain

Mary Magdalene

Wikimedia - Creative Commons Attribution-Share Alike 4.0
International

About the Author

Sylvia Binsfeld

Sylvia Binsfeld is an indie filmmaker whose goal is to produce creative, entertaining films that raise our consciousness and help heal our planet. Because children grow up in such a fast-paced culture these days and are constantly inundated with adult information, Sylvia was inspired to produce the award-winning, short fantasy film, Dorme, where a young child embarks on a mystical dreamland journey with an important task to complete before the night is done. Soon after, she authored the book, *Dorme: A Magical Dreamland Visit*—which, paired together with the Dorme lullaby film, is meant to bring back the innocent imagination Sylvia remembers from her childhood, along with messages of love, peace, safety, and connection, to be shared with a child before drifting to sleep.

Several years ago, Sylvia had a profound experience during a group sound healing session at a qigong intensive, which inspired years of research and the writing of this book. Sylvia also founded the Conscious Media Movement (CMM) at that time. CMM was put on hold while she finished writing. Now with the book completed, she will further the development of CMM, to support media makers in creating conscious media by offering guidance and spiritual development classes designed for filmmakers and storytellers.

Sylvia will also get back to the task of getting her next conscious media (family, fantasy) film *Upon a Starry Night* made.

About the Illustrator

Evangelia Philippidis

A match made in heaven. I discovered Evangelia Philippidis' soulful artwork when I googled "Holy Spirit Rising" in quotation marks on the internet, to see if there were any books out that already had that title. I didn't find any, but I did come across Evangelia's beautiful illustration, titled Holy Spirit Rising! I knew instantly, I was directed there for a reason and this was the perfect match for the book.

The beautiful illustration of the Holy Spirit rising with her flames, in her womanly form, graceful, loving, and dove-like, but with incredible power and strength, embodied everything I was writing! In incredible gratitude to the gifted artist Evangelia, this image now graces the front cover of this book! And it doesn't stop there. Evangelia had other gorgeous, meaningful images that were a fit. Thank you, Evangelia for blessing Holy Spirit Rising with your exquisite art!

https://www.theartofevangelia.net/hello

9 780983 704836